Exile of the Heart: A Memoir Across Three Continents

Copyright Rasheed Abou-Elsamh © 2025

All Rights Reserved

No part of this publication may be reproduced, distributed, or transmitted in any form or by any means, including photocopying, recording, artificial intelligence (AI) or other electronic or mechanical methods, without the prior written permission of the publisher, except in the case of brief quotations embodied in critical reviews.

ISBN 979-8-9938765-0-4

Cover design by Ifan Bates

EXILE OF THE HEART
A MEMOIR ACROSS THREE CONTINENTS

RASHEED ABOU-ELSAMH

STORY BRIDGE AGENCY

PREFACE

PREFACE

This book began as a way to make sense of everything I've lived through, across countries, careers, relationships, and faith. I didn't set out to write a memoir. I just started writing what I remembered. What hurt. What stayed with me. What changed me.

Some stories here are painful. Others are funny, strange, or tender. I've written about my childhood between Geneva, Cairo, and Brasilia; my college years in the U.S.; my time as a journalist in Saudi Arabia; and the deep love, and betrayal, I experienced with people I once trusted. You'll meet family, friends, lovers, and colleagues who shaped my life in ways I couldn't have predicted.

I've lived between cultures, between expectations, between truths. And like many of us who've straddled more than one identity, I've often felt like I belonged everywhere, and nowhere. Writing this book helped me put some of that confusion into words.

If you find a piece of your own story in these pages, something you've carried silently, I hope you'll feel less alone. That's the only real reason I've written this.

— Rasheed Abou-Elsamh

I

THE FALL OF LORENZO

BRASILIA, APRIL 2021

"Leave your mask on and don't take it off!"

Lorenzo's voice cracked through the humid air as we pulled away from the airport.

I had just returned from nearly two months in Houston, Texas, where I had stayed with my aunt and uncle to get my COVID-19 shots. It was April 23, 2021. Both Brazil and the U.S. were still gasping under the weight of the virus, and I, at 57, had jumped at the chance to get vaccinated early, instead of risking my life.

"You might've caught something on the flight. Shower the moment we get home," Lorenzo ordered, his words not so much concerned as a command.

The panic in his voice didn't register fully then. I was jet-lagged, still rolling in and out of airport haze. I had left Lorenzo taking care of my house and pets while I was away in the U.S. We'd done this before. He knew the routine.

He had gotten sick while I was away, at least that's what he said. But still everything seemed to be going fine when I suddenly got a video call from him, while I was visiting the Golden Gate bridge in San Francisco with my cousins.

"I got Covid! I'm in the hospital! I need money to pay the bill," pleaded Lorenzo from a hospital bed with oxygen tubes in his nostrils. "My lungs are bad. Please, Rasheed—I don't want to die. "Please help me!"

Stunned, I wired him the equivalent of $2,000 without a second thought. At the time, all I could hear was panic in his voice and see the oxygen tubes wrapped around his face. But later, friends of mine raised doubts. Some were convinced Lorenzo had faked the entire scene, the hospital bed, the tubes, even the fear in his voice, just to scam more money out of me. I didn't want to believe them. The seed of doubt had been planted, but I found their doubts hard to believe. The bed in the video looked like a real hospital bed, with the oxygen outlets on the wall behind him. And the panic in his voice didn't feel fake. Either he truly was in distress, or he was a very good actor.

I had met Lorenzo in October 2009, at a gay sauna in Brasilia while my mother was away visiting her sister in the U.S. He was 22; I was 45. I didn't have a car then, so after a few drinks, I asked if he could give me a ride home. He agreed without hesitation and zipped me across town in his tiny Chevrolet Celta, chatting nonstop and cracking jokes the entire way. I fell for him quickly. After that night, we began seeing each other regularly.

Lorenzo was six feet tall and had wonderfully thick biceps. He wasn't a gym rat, but he ran regularly and did work out with weights. We went to the tiny love motels that are found in most Brazilian cities, where the rooms are rented out by the hour, for couples who do not have an appropriate place for a tryst. They were as common as Brazilian cafezinhos.

We also met a coffee shops to sip our small cups of strong coffee accompanied by fizzy mineral water on the side and often a pastry. We talked about politics, both Brazilian and foreign, economics, movies and TV shows that we liked. And we made each other laugh often.

But I had no idea that our relationship was about to take a sharp turn for the worse, on that fateful ride home from the airport, with Lorenzo at the wheel.

When we pulled up to my house, I stepped out and opened the back door to grab my hand luggage.

"Leave everything and go take a shower right away! I will bring your things in," Lorenzo shouted. But the moment I stepped into my living room, I knew something was off. My desktop computer was smashed across my desk. "What happened?!" I asked, my
voice rising.

"I wrecked your computer in a fit of anger," Lorenzo admitted. "I'll buy you a new one," he added showing little remorse.

"Where are my armchairs?" I asked, scanning the empty spaces where they used to sit.

"Oh, I spilled some drinks on them, so I took them to be cleaned," he replied casually.

I went into my bedroom and undressed to take a quick shower, though a terrible sense of foreboding clung to me. Something didn't feel right. After the shower, when I came back to the living room, all the lights were on, but Lorenzo was gone.

My suitcases were nowhere to be seen. I looked in the back of my Subaru Forester and there was nothing. Thiago vanished with everything including my hand luggage, which had my passports and an expensive ring that I deeply cherished.

. . .

I called him immediately and asked where my things were.

"I didn't take your stuff. I left your suitcases under some bushes near your house," he said, a bizarre nonsensical excuse that made no sense at all.

I walked over to my mother's house to check on my two dogs, Penny and Nelly. The moment I entered the kitchen I was struck by the horrible mess that Lorenzo had left behind. My mom's refrigerator was gone, and all the food that had been inside was now dumped carelessly across the countertops.

I called out to the dogs as I opened the door to the area where they slept at night. A wave of urine and feces stink hit my eyes and nostrils, and my bedraggled dogs came running to me. Poor Penny had lost so much weight that her ribs were visible. Nelly's coat was filthy and matted. It was a heartbreaking sight.

While in the hospital, Lorenzo assured me that one of his assistants was visiting my house every day to feed the dogs and cats. But their condition told a very different story. They looked like they hadn't eaten for several days.

I walked down the hall to my mother's bedroom. The door, which I had locked before leaving, was wide open. Her papers and clothes were piled up on her bed. Her makeup table was gone, and all her jewelry was gone.

Stunned, I called Lorenzo again and shouted about the missing jewelry. "It was Marcos! He ransacked the house," he claimed, mentioning a friend of mine. But I told him that couldn't be true. There were no signs of forced entry on any of the doors or windows, and only Lorenzo had keys to my house.

Shocked and desperate, I went to my neighbor's house and told them what had happened.

"Did you see any moving truck taking things out of my home?" I asked.

"No, we didn't notice anything strange," they said.

I asked them to call me an Uber, as I couldn't get the main gate open to our property as Lorenzo had taken the remote control for it with him.

I went straight to my friend Gitty's apartment and asked her to come with me to the local police station so I could file a complaint against Lorenzo. She kindly took me to the station in her car and then brought me back home afterward. The police did not seem particularly concerned about my situation, and to this day, they have failed to recover any of my mother's missing jewelry.

Years later, after I had moved to Houston, Lorenzo would call me and tell me that he had my ring and watch, and that he could return them to me. He even mentioned my mother's jewelry, saying he still had it and could return it to me.

I never believed him, sure that he had sold most of it to a pawnshop. I knew it was the classic move of a narcissist, that Lorenzo was, to try and suck me back into his life. I declined.

2

MOTHER, MEMORY, AND LOSS

My mother, Joyce Alice Storkson, passed away on December 14, 2019, after a botched heart procedure at the Hospital Sírio-Libanês in Brasilia. She was 83 years old. Apart from a heart condition, she was remarkably healthy and energetic. She went for walks every day and continued going to the gym well into r seventies.

Born in 1936, my mother was shaped by the Great Depression and the post–World War II American boom. Like my father, she was frugal with money and disliked anything flashy. One of her greatest achievements was helping her father build their family home in O'Fallon, Missouri, something she spoke of often. She was practical, no-nonsense, and deeply optimistic.

I grew up very attached to her. As a young boy in Geneva, Switzerland, I loved sitting on her lap and going out shopping with her at the supermarket. She was also an excellent baker, she taught me how to bake cookies, cakes and brownies.

My father was rather absent during my childhood, always working at his office or on work trips. I'm sure he didn't like how close I was to my mother. Perhaps he feared I was becoming too feminine. In an effort to "toughen me up," my parents enrolled me in judo lessons when I was eight. I didn't enjoy it. I made it to a yellow belt before I dropped out.

My father was Saudi, originally from Cairo, Egypt. He had been sent to study the U.S. telephone system in the 1950s by the Saudi government but switched to International Relations at American University in Washington, D.C., earning both bachelor's and master's degrees.

My mother left the small-town of O'Fallon as soon as she could in the mid-1950s. After passing the Civil Service Exam, she quickly found a job as a secretary at the State Department in Washington. It was a fine job, as my mother wanted to see the world, and would later marry my father, who himself would become a diplomat. They met at a party hosted at the International House for Students. They dated and soon got married in Virginia and had my sister Jamelah in January 1959. I came along five years later.

3
THE RED EARTH OF BRASILIA

BRASILIA, 1975-1980

As the Pan Am Boeing 707 descended into Brasília on September 4, 1975, we stared out the jet's windows at a surreal scene of red dirt and dust.

My father had already started his new post as the Saudi Cultural Attaché. My mother stayed behind in Geneva with Jamelah and I, packing up our Danish furniture and photo albums alone and storing everything.

Unlike European ones, the Saudi government did not offer a cargo stipend for diplomats to move their belongings between posts. Years later, after my father had begrudgingly paid storage fees for far too long, we realized we'd never recover our childhood photos and sentimental belongings.

We were all relatively young. My dad was 49, my mom was 39, I was 11, and my sister was 16. Brasília felt completely alien to us, new, isolated, unfamiliar. Designed by famous Brazilian architect Oscar Niemeyer, and urban planner Lucio Costa, the old dream of moving Brazil's capital away from the Atlantic coastline and into the middle of the country, had finally been done by President Juscelino Kubitschek. He broke ground in 1956, and the city was inaugurated just 41 months later in April 1960.

An ultra-modern city rose out of the Planalto Central, a plateau around 1,300 meters above sea level. Workers were brought in from the Brazilian Northeast to build the city, and all the construction materials, such as steel and concrete, had to be flown or trucked in.

You either love Brasília or you hate it. Brazilians love to complain that the capital lacks the vibrancy of São Paulo and the beaches of Rio de Janeiro.

When we arrived, we all hated Brasilia. There was red dust everywhere, and the city had hardly any trees. Accustomed to the old-world charm of Geneva and Europe, the sheer frontier-ness of Brasilia was shocking. Little did we know that, forty years later, my mother and I would come to love it.

We first lived in a small, rented house in the Lago Sul, a stucco box with a corrugated roof. We all detested the house, but our parents told us to be patient and that we would eventually move to a nicer home.

The supermarkets were bleak, like something out of communist Eastern Europe. Brazil was following a strict nationalist, no-imports economic policy, so we had no foreign goods to buy whatsoever.

The available bread was white and boring, milk was sold in plastic bags, and the rice and beans we bought to cook had to be picked over for tiny stones and possible bugs. Flash forward 50 years, and Brazil's supermarkets nowadays are a far cry from those we encountered in 1975.

Jamelah and I were promptly enrolled in the Escola Americana de Brasilia (EAB), the only English-language school in town. I was in the 6th grade, Miss Sheridan's class, and my sister was in 11th grade.

Founded in the late 1960s for the children of US and other diplomats in Brasilia, the school was very small, with approximately 600 students from kindergarten to 12th grade. Most of our teachers were young Americans who came to Brazil on short two-year contracts to teach at EAB. Some stayed a bit longer, but there was a large turnover of American teachers.

It was at EAB that I learned to speak, read and write Portuguese, as per Brazilian law, my school had to teach the language to all its students.

It was a fantastic education in the Portuguese language and Brazilian history and culture in general, taught to us by Brazilian teachers such as Celinda Soares, who is my friend until this day. Their lessons served me so well, that many decades later I was hired to write a regular column on the Middle East for *O Globo*, one of Brazil's largest daily newspapers. Friends would ask me if I was writing my column in English and the paper translating it into Portuguese, to which I replied with relish: "No, I write my columns in Portuguese!"

My classmates in the sixth grade hailed from all over the world. Some of the nationalities represented were the USA, South Africa, Nigeria, Yugoslavia, South Korea, West Germany, and Israel. Of course, these were all the children of diplomats posted in Brasilia. There were some Brazilian students, too, usually the children of diplomats who had studied abroad in English or of wealthy businessmen.

Years later in high school, the daughter of the Iraqi ambassador to Brazil invited our whole class to her birthday party at their residence. When we arrived we were confronted by a huge photograph of the dictator Saddam Hussein in their living room, at least eight feet tall, grinning down at us while we danced to pop tunes. It was a surreal sight.

Some of the more interesting students were children of American missionaries from the Summer Institute of Linguistics. These missionaries traveled to remote areas of the Amazon jungle, where they lived among Indigenous tribes and often created a written language for those who did not have one, to be able to translate the Bible into their language, teach it to them, and ultimately convert them to Christianity.

But by the late 1970s, Brazil's military dictatorship decided they did not want these gringo missionaries running around the Amazon unimpeded, so they were asked to leave the country.

4
THE LIBRARY AND THE CLOSET

The small library that we had at EAB became my sanctuary as a somewhat nerdy and reserved student. There, I loved to read the American magazines that the school subscribed to and received via the US Embassy APO mail service.

Foreign Affairs, *The New Republic*, and *The Atlantic* were my favorites. I would often borrow them and take them home for further reading. The library also subscribed to *House and Garden*, *Good Housekeeping* and *Glamour* magazines, which I regularly took home for my mother and Jamelah to read. These provided a lifeline to American baking recipes, which pleased my mother, and through her baking, the rest of us too.

EAB was, therefore, a little beacon of American education and culture. I still remember my American classmates whose parents worked at the U.S. Embassy bringing Pringles and Tootsie Rolls for lunch and occasionally sharing them with the rest of us, who didn't have access to such goods.

Rejane, who was Brazilian, was my favorite librarian at EAB. She always chatted with me and let me borrow the latest magazines overnight as long as I promised to return them the next morning. My

Brazilian American friend Ricky Seabra used to always make fun of her name, asking me how "Re-jane" was doing.

Today, 50 years later, I'm still friends with Ricky and we talk on WhatsApp several times a week. He came out as gay much later than I did, after attending the Parsons School of Design in New York.

"You were the 'out' one at EAB, with your femininity and crushes on older guys," Ricky told me recently. "Don't you remember you sent a note to a guy you liked, and we were shocked and scared that the guy might hit you. But he talked to you and gently turned you down."

I had forgotten about that incident, but I do remember being bullied at EAB by fellow students who called me "bicha", a derogatory Portuguese slang expression similar to

fag.

All through high school, I didn't hang out with the jocks and wasn't invited to any of the parties that students held on weekends. With my father's restrictions that Jamelah and I couldn't go to parties at night or sleep over at friends' houses, being excluded from such extracurricular activities didn't really bother me. I was content with going to see film classics such as "A Streetcar Named Desire" with my parents at the Casa Thomas Jefferson on Saturday nights, or baking brownies and lemon squares on Sundays.

Looking back now, I can see the many clues that showed that I was indeed a teenager coming to terms with his sexuality. Brazil is an intensely macho society, and a very sensual one too. Brazilians love hugging and kissing each other. Although the military dictatorship banned hardcore pornographic movies, *pornochanchadas* were not. They were salacious comedies shown on Brazilian television after midnight on the weekends, titillating stories that showed only the breasts of female actresses, with no penetration allowed. It was "porn lite", a sort of Canterbury Tales updated for the 1970s.

I used to watch these films, more out of curiosity than a desire to see naked women. Around the age of 15, I started secretly buying issues of the Brazilian edition of *Playboy* magazine. The magazine was widely available on newsstands across Brasilia, and celebrities would pride themselves when the magazine invited them to pose for its pages and front cover. I would eagerly leaf through them, but then one day, when an issue featured a photo essay with a man and woman, I suddenly noticed that I was turned on more by the man in the pictures than the woman. This led me to buy American gay porn magazines such as *Blueboy*, which were imported and sold at the airport newsstand. This is when I discovered that there was a gay community out there, and a sexual world where men loved other men without any shame.

I also started buying the only gay Brazilian magazine at the time, *Rose*. It was the smaller size of a *Reader's Digest* and had some erotic photos, stories, and advice columns. At the back was a pen pal section, where one could find other gay men who wanted to meet for sex and friendship. This was way before the advent of the internet and the cellphone. I was too young to go out to bars to meet other gay men, so finding them in the magazine was the next best thing. That is where I met Alison (in Brazil, Alison is a male name). I sent him a letter in response to his ad and soon got a reply with his address, phone number, and a tentative date to meet at his apartment. I was terrified at the thought of meeting him but felt compelled to follow through to see if men were what I liked.

Alison turned out to be a kind and sweet person and became a lifelong friend of mine, with whom I am in contact to this day.

5
THE DAY JAMELAH DISAPPEARED

The morning of January 24, 1980, was sunny and beautiful. It was summer in Brasilia, Brazil, and the sky was a deep blue. My sister and I had breakfast together at our dining table in our family's apartment in SQS 305, bloco E, on the fourth floor.

A wall of windows ran along the dining and living room areas. It was all one big area with no walls separating the two areas. The same windows through which our Siamese cat Sesame once jumped through while chasing an insect. He landed on the strip of grass that separated our building from the cars parked out front. I remember rushing down in a panic to rescue Sesame, worried that he might have suffered an internal injury and would bleed to death. As soon as I found him on the grass, dazed but apparently not worse for the wear. I scooped him up and kissed his cheek. In return, probably because he was still spooked from the fall, he scratched both sides of my face with his claws and jumped down.

"Oow!" I screamed, momentarily stunned, "you little shit!" He didn't stay much longer with us after that, as we gave him to some friends, and we didn't hear what happened to him after that.

. . .

Jamelah had already graduated from EAB and was studying Fine Arts at the University of Brasilia. My father had bought her a Brasilia Volkswagen station wagon, which she drove to the campus every week day. What she was doing there, apart from going to classes, none of us knew. She would come home in the late afternoon. One of her teachers was Kathleen Sidki, an American artist from St. Louis, Missouri, married to Said Sidki, a Palestinian math professor at the same university.

Brazilian university campuses have long been hotbeds of leftist activists, and UnB was no different. During the early years of the military dictatorship, which started in April 1964 and lasted until 1985, students would regularly protest on campus against the government-imposed censorship and restrictions on freedom of thought and gathering. Jamelah was clearly influenced by them, coming home one day and declaring to me that our father was "bourgeois" because he owned a Mercedes-Benz.

The truth was that my father had imported a Mercedes that he resold to a Brazilian buyer. At the time, only diplomats could import cars into Brazil, so they fetched high prices because of their scarcity.

Kathleen and Said were already friends of my parents, and their two kids were our friends. They would come over to visit us on the weekend, and we would visit them at their house in the Lago Norte. I remember listening to the Carpenters with their kids, enjoying and soaking in the melancholic voice of Karen Carpenter singing "We've Only Just Begun."

But back to that fateful day. Jamelah dropped me off that morning at the American School. She acted totally normal. No apparent stress or worry. "See you later," she said as I hopped out of her car. That was the last time I would ever see her again. I was 15 and in the 10th grade.

Later that afternoon, when I was already home, a folded piece of watercolor paper was slipped under our front door. I picked it up as soon as I noticed it and read Jamelah's familiar handwriting saying in part:

"I have decided to run away as I can no longer live with any of you.

"Mom has always been mean to me, making me clean the kitchen floor in Switzerland. And she has shown that she clearly favors you Rasheed over me."

I was stunned and immediately gave it to my mother to read.

We were all surprised, to say the least, as Jamelah had never hinted to us that she was so unhappy as to need to run away to safeguard her happiness. My parents never mistreated us, and they gave us a comfortable life. Sure, my dad had joked a few times that Jamelah should marry one of her male cousins in Saudi Arabia, but that was only because he had grown up with that tradition. I don't think he was going to force us to do that. After all, he had completely bucked Arab and Islamic traditions by marrying my mother, a Christian American. He certainly didn't practice what he preached.

But Jamelah was having nothing of this. Apparently egged on by leftist friends at the university, and by Kathleen also, to run away and be "free" in the United States, she followed their advice. It all seemed so cold-hearted to me, especially when I saw how deeply hurt and embarrassed my parents were with her disappearance.

I too was very upset and sad. I didn't know how to process my sister's disappearance. I didn't have any friends or teachers that I could talk to about this. I remember I had a midterm Algebra test a few days after her disappearance, and feeling too embarrassed to ask my teacher permission to take the test later, I took the test even though I had not been able to study for it. I naturally got a bad grade.

My father went to the police to report Jamelah missing, but they said they couldn't do anything if Jamelah didn't want to be found as she was 21 years old. Next, he went to see the consul general at the US Embassy and found out that Jamelah had indeed renewed her US passport at the embassy in November, and that a man had accompanied her. Who was this man? We never found out.

My parents also called all of Jamelah's friends from the university, to ask if they knew where she was. All denied knowing anything about my sister's whereabouts or future plans. This total lack of information, and not fully understanding her motivations, was very hard to handle. At least if she had a heated argument with us in person, we could have counter argued her feelings of alleged neglect.

But something in me did not believe Kathleen and Said's vehement insistence that they didn't know anything about Jamelah running away. When I went away to college in the US, I remember writing a letter to Kathleen accusing her of knowing where my sister was. Of course, I never heard back. And we never heard from Jamelah for 22 years. Was she still alive? Ill? Married? Become a mother? We did not know.

Then in January 2002, my parents received a long-distance phone call early in the morning from Michigan. "Jamelah is very ill with cancer, and we thought you should know," one of my sister's friends told my parents. At the time I was still working at *Arab News* in Jeddah, and when my parents told me I was shocked but somehow relieved. "At least she's still alive," I said to myself.

We soon found out that Jamelah had been married, was living in Grand Rapids, Michigan, and had a teenage son called Alex. She was divorced now and had breast cancer. Sadly, the cancer had spread in her body, after she had initially resisted having chemotherapy, and tried "alternative medicine" first. My mother's sisters, Clara and Linda, went to see Jamelah in Michigan, and reported back to my mother. My mother refused to go, telling me "I'll only go if Jamelah asks me too." I thought that was a bit harsh, but I could also understand my parents' anger at being kept in the dark for over two decades. Couldn't Jamelah have in the interim sent my parents an email saying she was okay and that they were now grandparents?

I eventually got Jamelah's email address and started corresponding with her, asking about her life, and telling her about mine.

. . .

"I am sorry to have not been around to see you grow up. I feel like I left right at a point when we probably could have become good friends and joined forces to make things come out more to our liking," she wrote to me on July 5, 2002.

"Someday I will write to our parents. I feel badly about not having a relationship with mother," she wrote in the same email. "I just cannot abide the thought of dealing with our father. I just have too many strong beliefs about women that I won't give up…and life is too short to allow people to rain on one's parade."

I wrote back saying I wanted to come visit her in Michigan as soon as possible, but she asked to wait until she was better.

"Hey, you can't come visit me until I'm really well and my life is somewhat back to normal," she wrote me on July 17, 2002. "It would stress me out incredibly to not be with it and have you come. I'm a highly stressable person when I'm not able to function at full tilt. There was one time when I was on chemo and it was wigging me out something terrible, so I ended up asking my guardian angel friends Sarah and Joel not to come over for some time because I wasn't well and I could not bear them having to deal with me in that state. …So be patient, I'll let you know when I'm ready."

When I asked if she remembered our time together growing up, she replied that of course she did.

"But you know, I really think that you and I have very different memories of how things were, and I'm sorry, there are good memories, but overall, I don't remember much," she wrote me. "I feel that I have learned that I had so much potential that I was never allowed to pursue, perhaps that's why I don't spend time on memories. …Our parents are good people in and of themselves, and they did great things for us, but in my mind, things were not exactly of a positive, pro-active nature."

. . .

Sadly, I never made it over to Michigan to see Jamelah when she was still alive. In May 2003 she succumbed to her cancer and passed away. Her body was cremated and her ashes spread in places that she loved. She was only 43 years old, and Alex was 15. It would take another 12 years before my mother and I were able to finally personally meet Alex at a family reunion in St. Charles, Missouri.

6

THE AMERICAN DREAM, DELAYED

In my junior year in high school, I applied to six or seven universities and colleges in the U.S. I had done relatively well on my SAT scores, especially on the verbal section, and was accepted at three schools: Swarthmore College, a small, liberal arts Quaker school near Philadelphia; Georgetown University in Washington, D.C.; and Hampshire College in rural Massachusetts.

The Hampshire College brochure was attractive, with inspiring words and pictures of the beautiful campus and classrooms. Their education philosophy was very progressive; with no grades, only detailed written evaluations from professors, a radical concept born of the 1960s free-thought movement. My mother wanted nothing to do with it. "You can't go to a school where they don't grade you!" she exclaimed, horrified.

That left me with Swarthmore and Georgetown. The Catholic school did not appeal to me, despite it being in my natal city. It was too big for me, I thought, used to the small scale of EAB. Swarthmore, with its progressive politics, small size, and the Quaker support of Palestinian rights, was what swayed me in the end. And being in the suburbs, it was only a short train ride away from Philadelphia if I needed to go to the big city for shopping or culture.

Luckily, my father promised to get me a scholarship from the Saudi government to pay for my tuition, room and board. But there was only one catch: Once I was accepted at Swarthmore, I had to defer my admission for a year and study Arabic in Saudi Arabia. It was a Faustian bargain that I didn't want. But I had no choice if I wanted to pursue my American dream of finding a gay life at college and in a society where it was okay to be homosexual and wasn't against the law.

The summer after I graduated from high school in 1982, my Aunt Samiha came to visit us in Brasilia along with her sarcastic husband, daughter and son. They stayed in our small guest house at our *chácara* in the Lago Sul. The reason for their visit: my aunt was having a fat removal procedure on her stomach, and my female cousin a nose job.

Both procedures were successful, but the recovery was slow. Eventually, my uncle and cousins returned earlier to Jeddah, leaving behind my aunt, who needed a few more weeks of recovery before she was medically cleared for air travel. My father decided I would travel back with her to Saudi Arabia to begin the process of enrolling at King Abdulaziz University in Jeddah for Arabic studies.

I remember flying through Paris on Air France with my aunt on a tiring journey to Jeddah. When we arrived, I was given a room in their apartment, and I sunk into a deep depression as the realization of what I was facing for the next academic year became clearer. It was my first time away from my parents, and I was unhappy.

I remember listening to Carly Simon's "Torch" album on repeat, her sad lyrics a perfect reflection of how I felt as my relatives decamped to their beach house for the weekend. I refused to go, staying back and wallowing in my sorrow of having my American dream postponed. I listened nonstop to "Blue of Blue," "I Get Along Without You Very Well," "Hurt," and "What Shall I Do With This Child?"

My uncle had built the six-story apartment building at the end of Madares Street (Schools Street in Arabic, named for all the nearby educational institutions) in the Baghdadiyah Gharbiah district. It was close to Madinah Road, Jeddah's main North-South thoroughfare, and to Balad, the old and historic center of Jeddah. He was proud of having installed a garbage chute in the building, inspired by the one in our Geneva apartment.

After a few weeks, I moved into my grandmother's two-story villa a few streets away. My *teita* lived upstairs; my Uncle Anas and his family lived on the ground floor. I had my own small room. Since I didn't yet know how to drive—and no one offered to lend me a driver, I had to take the public Saptco buses, with their small walled-off sections in the back reserved for female passengers.

I soon learned how to take the buses from where I lived to the university campus.

I had once or twice slummed it by taking the much smaller private mini-buses that zipped around the city, their folding doors permanently shoved open, their insides stuffed with commuters, with some hanging out of the doors.

In these we were jammed up to one another, making it a field day for pickpockets. On one such occasion, when I jumped off the bus at my destination, I patted the left pocket of my thobe only to find my black wallet, and a good amount of money, missing.

After that I never took a smaller bus again.

To get to the Saptco buses that ran on Madinah Road, I had to walk up from our house for around ten minutes. I had started my internship at the *Arab News* newspaper, and one day returning from the paper at night I noticed a large white American car following me. The driver was a young Saudi man, who leered at me and yelled if I wanted to join him in his car.

I was at once terrified, but also a little flattered, of this brazen sexual approach. I started running, and the car followed me. I ran into an apartment building, and breathless, went up the stairs to the first floor, hoping the man wouldn't follow me into the building.

I wasn't a virgin anymore, but I wasn't ready to begin having sexual assignations with strangers in the street.

After around 15 minutes, I snuck down the stairs and out of the building, looking to see if the man was still there waiting for me. But he wasn't. He had left to look for another prey somewhere else, and I continued walking home, thankful that I had escaped from the man.

King Abdul Aziz University, or KAAU for short, had a large campus and had a foreign student population of Muslim students for whom the Saudi government gave scholarships to study in the Kingdom. Most didn't speak Arabic, so an intensive Arabic course was put into place to teach them the language in which all the classes were held.

I joined a small class of international students, many from what was then Zaire. Strangely, all our teachers were Sudanese, friendly, competent, and gifted in teaching Arabic.

I struggled only with the Qur'anic surahs we were assigned to interpret in Arabic. I once took one home and asked my Aunt Samira to help explain it. Even she was stumped.

On the weekends, the only entertainment available were shopping malls, as cinemas were recently banned in the Kingdom. The most popular one was Jeddah International Market on Madinah Road. There, you could find cafés, jewelry and clothing stores, electronics stores, a small bookstore selling newspapers and magazines, and a supermarket.

The mall had little water-feature ponds with live turtles in them, and I used to go there to buy copies of the *International Herald Tribun*e and British newspapers such as *The Times of London* and *The Guardian*. Of course, these publications were regularly sold with pages torn out or images covered with black ink. This was the work of the censors employed by Al-Khazindar, the largest importer of foreign publications, which was under strict orders of the Ministry of Information to cover up revealing photos of women and tear out articles critical of Saudi Arabia.

This was before the internet. Communication with the outside world meant expensive international phone calls or slow-moving letters. Reading censored news was the only glimpse we had of the wider world.

The other big draw of Jeddah International Market were the music stores that sold cassette tapes of all the most popular Arab and Western singers. The Kingdom had not yet signed any international copyright treaties, so all the music available was in fact bootlegged versions of original albums. The sound quality was excellent, however the artwork of the album covers was often changed to remove images deemed offensive in Saudi Arabia.

7
INTERNING AT ARAB NEWS

I probably have my parents to thank for becoming a journalist. From the earliest age, I saw both of them reading newspapers. My mother read the *International Herald Tribune* while we lived in Geneva, and my father read Saudi newspapers sent to him by his ministry.

My mom would often send me to the newspaper and tobacco shop up the hill from our apartment in Le Lignon, Geneva, to buy a copy of the *IHT* and a pack of Dunhill red cigarettes. She would sit with the paper, doing the crossword, and I would read it too. At the time, it was co-owned by *The New York Times* and *Washington Post*, which meant that it had articles from both papers.

When we moved to Brazil in 1975, there was no *IHT* to read, and we were decades away from having the internet or even dreaming that we would have access to it in the future.

In Brasilia, we would read the local paper, the *Correio Braziliense*. Then in the late 70s and early 80s, my father started receiving regular shipments of Saudi newspapers via the diplomatic pouch. Among them were two English-language papers: *Arab News* and

Saudi Gazette. I would read both papers and eventually wrote a letter to the editor-in chief of *Arab News*, Khaled Almaeena, saying how much I liked the paper and asking if I could intern at the paper when I spent my academic year in Jeddah learning Arabic.

He wrote back and said I could intern at the paper, to look him up when I arrived in Jeddah.

I still remember my first visit to *Arab News* in 1982. It was squeezed into the second floor of a somewhat rundown and dusty building in the Al-Sharafiah neighborhood of Jeddah. Khaled was all smiles when he met me. The paper was founded in 1975 and was only seven years old.

By 1983, *Arab News* had moved to a brand-new building in the Al-Faisaliah district. The building was the headquarters of Saudi Research and Publishing Company, and all of its publications had their offices there. *Arab News, Alsharq al-Awsat, Al-Muslimoon, AlMajala* magazine, *Sayidaty* magazine, and *Saudi Business* all had staff here. In the basement was a giant printing press. We'd hear its thunderous rumble echoing through the building every evening. Later, an annex was added to house even bigger presses. I would go in several times a week and collect stories from the various news agency teletype machines, which clanged furiously when a breaking news story was coming through.

Editors would edit the stories on the printouts and then send them to be typeset. Large strips of thick wax paper, containing each story, were printed out and given to the page makers. The sub-editors would draw the layout of each page, showing the page makers where each headline, story, photo, and ad went. Then they would watch the page makers lay out each page, using hot blue wax rolled on the back of each strip of paper with the stories on them, and attach them to the page. When the page was ready, it was sent to be photographed, with the resulting pictures being burned into metal sheets from which the paper would be printed.

Nowadays, everything is computerized, with software such as

InDesign, used to digitally make the pages and send them off to be printed.

To say that groups of Indian and Pakistani journalists ran *Arab News* and *Saudi Gazette*, would not be an overstatement. Both papers had experimented employing American and British journalists, but they had better success with Subcontinental ones. Farouk Luqman was the managing editor of *Arab News*. He was a bubbly man originally from Aden, Yemen, who loved everything Indian. He spoke Urdu and adored Indian food and culture. He was also a graduate of the Columbia School of Journalism and an excellent journalist.

Khaled came from Saudi Arabian Airlines and loved to tell people that the publishers and founders of *Arab News*, Hisham and Ali Hafez, had hired him for his excellent command of English and good looks. Khaled would be my boss, on and off, for the next 24 years.

There was a small rivalry between the two. Having lived and studied there, Khaled loved Pakistan, and Farouk was pro-India. We on staff were like children caught between divorced parents. If we couldn't get a story approved by one, we'd go to the other. It made the newsroom lively, and in the end, helped produce solid journalism.

During my 1982–83 internship, *Arab News* paid me a modest stipend every month for my work. I even managed to save up enough to buy my mother a gold Cartier Trinity ring from Jeddah International Market.

It was while interning at *Arab News* that I met Philip Shehadi, an American reporter for *Saudi Business*. He was also gay, so we became friends. I often went up to the third floor to chat with him at night. Philip later left *Saudi Business* and joined Reuters as a correspondent.

In March 1991, while he was based in Algiers, he was murdered in his apartment, apparently killed by a man he had met.

Philip was originally from Princeton, New Jersey, and had

studied at Oberlin College. He spoke Arabic fluently and was a rising star at Reuters at 33.

His death shocked and saddened me. Was this the fate of every gay man, I thought to myself. I was still a neophyte in the gay world, and did not have anyone in Jeddah with whom I could discuss such taboo subjects.

8
BACK IN THE NEWSROOM

I graduated from Swarthmore College in 1987 with a BA in Political Science. That summer, I moved to Washington, D.C. and rented a room in an all-black neighborhood. I had followed my friend Michael North there, and we often met to have meals together or go to the movies.

I found a job as a salesman at a small and rather commercial bookstore near Dupont Circle. One day, the bestselling author Tom Clancy came into the store and looked at the books of his that we were selling. He was pretty gruff with me, frowning the whole time, and had the nerve to buy a pack of gum with a credit card! So American of him, I thought at the time.

I was making minimum wage then, which was certainly not enough to live on decently. I remember I could hardly pay for a $5 sandwich for lunch when I worked at the bookstore. Luckily, I had some money left over from my Swarthmore scholarship, which helped tide me over through the summer. But come Fall, and I found myself without my job at the bookstore, with the owner telling me I didn't have the right "attitude"! I wonder what attitude he expected for the wage of $ 6.35 an hour.

My father kept pressuring me to move to Saudi Arabia, claiming it was my duty to "repay" my Saudi government scholarship by working in Saudi Arabia. I resisted as long as I could and now find it strange now that I did not even try to get a job at *The Washington Post*. I think it was because I didn't have an experienced journalist mentor in Washington to give me good advice and guide me in the right direction.

I finally gave in to my father and flew to London from New York in December 1987, where I met him. We then flew on to Jeddah to begin my 20-year adventure of living and working in Saudi.

9
IKEA FURNITURE, BIG DECISIONS

My dad soon found an apartment for me in my uncle Abdulrazak's building, the one with the garbage shute, and we went to IKEA to furnish my new home with a bed, mattress, sofas, a dining table, and chairs. We also bought an American refrigerator and an electric Whirlpool stove.

I had two choices as a journalist in Saudi Arabia: work for *Saudi Gazette* or *Arab News*.

My father got an appointment with the editor-in-chief of *Saudi Gazette*, Ridah Larry. I found him rather formal and distant during our meeting. We then met with Hisham Ali Hafez, one of the publishers of *Arab News*. Both newspapers offered me positions, as at the time Saudis who spoke fluent English and wrote well were rare. I chose to accept *Arab News'* offer since I felt the most comfortable with its editor-in-chief Khaled Almaeena and had already worked there as in intern in 1982-83.

An experienced Indian editor called Pakkar Koya was assigned to train me. He taught me how to edit stories and how to lay out pages. He was from Kerala and was the editor of the Op-Ed page. He wore a drab daily uniform of a button-down, long-sleeve white shirt and dark brown slacks. Most of the staff were either Indian or Pakistani. *Arab News* had tried Western editors, but they found adapting to the culturally conservative society too difficult. The sub-continental editors on the other hand were mainly Muslim and earning wages they could never make back home. They kept to themselves and found that living in Saudi was not so difficult after all.

Almaeena liked me and often sent me on press junkets. My first was to India, where the Tea Board of India hosted a group of Gulf journalists. We traveled from Bombay to New Delhi, then to Agra, Calcutta, Bangalore, and finally to a tea plantation in the hills of Karnataka near the Kerala border.

When I returned, I wrote a lengthy article, and it was published in *Arab News* with pictures that I had taken. The young Saudi journalist representing *Saudi Gazette* on the same trip spoke poor English and, from what I could tell, didn't write well either. A few weeks later, leafing through the most recent edition of the *Saudi Gazette,* I found an article about the India trip by said journalist, who had copied my entire article verbatim and plastered his name on it!

This was long before the internet and social media, so I had no way of publicly shaming the plagiarist. I showed the piece to Almaeena, expecting outrage. Instead, he laughed and said, "Copying is the highest form of flattery."

I continued to fume at the journalist with no morals. Years later he was promoted to a high supervisory position in the Okaz organization, the mother company of *Saudi Gazette* and the Arabic daily *Okaz.*

10

CENSORS AND CLEAVAGE: LIFE AT ARAB NEWS

One of the first things I learned while editing stories was that Jerusalem could not be referred to as only that. We had to insert "Occupied Jerusalem" in datelines and stories that mentioned the ancient and disputed city. At first, I didn't understand why this was so important, but over the years I came to appreciate just how politically charged every word in the Middle East could be.

We didn't have government censors physically sitting in the newsroom, but the Ministry of Information closely watched everything we published. They were our invisible editors, ever-present and always watching.

Censorship at *Arab News* was legendary. Any wire story that criticized Saudi Arabia and/or the royal family was either not used or heavily edited.

The most infamous act of censorship happened in the first three days of the Iraqi invasion of Kuwait, that started on Aug. 2, 1990. No Saudi media outlet was allowed to report what was happening right next door to us. The Saudi government froze in fear, not knowing how to react. But most people had access to satellite TV, and CNN was reporting the invasion. It certainly made the country look like it was an ostrich sticking its head into a hole, in the vain hope that the harsh reality would simply disappear.

The invasion led to the US sending troops, warships and planes to Saudi Arabia to defend the Kingdom from a crazed Iraqi President Saddam Hussein, who while lobbing Scud missiles at Riyadh and Dammam, seemed like he might invade Saudi at any moment.

The presence of hundreds of thousands of infidel American troops in what many Muslims consider the holy lands of Saudi Arabia, would eventually prove to be one of the main motivators for Osama Bin Ladin to turn against the United States and the Saudi state with his Al-Qaeeda group of fighters.

But throughout the Gulf War and afterwards our self-censorship continued. Our editor in chief would get regular phone calls from the ministry complaining about such and such story or photograph. He would have to calm them down, explain the "mistake," and if the issue was serious enough, reprimand the page editor and proof-readers for letting it through. One of the strangest parts of the job was censoring photographs of Western female entertainers. If a woman's dress was too short or her neckline too low, we had to alter the image. In the beginning, it looked quite crude, but with the advent of Photoshop, we got better at covering up cleavage and bare legs. It still looked strange most of the time, but we felt it was the only way we could print the photograph.

The censors of imported magazines and newspapers were rather more crude. They would literally rip out whole pages containing "dangerous" articles, or ink over photographs of women deemed immodest. Sometimes, entire issues of *The Economist* or *Newsweek* were banned from entering the country if they featured a negative cover story about Saudi Arabia.

Travelers returning from abroad weren't exempt. Saudi Customs agents closely inspected any magazines, books, or movies brought into the country at the airport. I remember once having the page torn out of a *GQ* magazine I had brought back because it had a semi-naked woman pictured in an ad for men's perfume.

Imported movies were also heavily censored. Any kissing and sex scenes were cut, leading to some extraordinary films. Violence, on the other hand, was acceptable, which I always found strange and objectionable.

II
FINDING MYSELF AT SWARTHMORE

When I was finally allowed to start attending Swarthmore College in the autumn of 1983, one year after my original start date, I immediately sought out the campus student group for LGBTQ+ students: The Gay and Lesbian Union. At the very first meeting, I met fellow freshman Michael North and we quickly became best friends. Michael was from St. Louis, Missouri, and this gave us something in common as my mother was also from Missouri. He was also wickedly funny.

We became inseparable. Although we were studying for completely different majors, he was studying Classics and I was in Political Science, we ate most meals together in the smaller dining rooms of Sharples. The main hall was where the jocks and more conventional students gathered. The side rooms were for the artsy, the nerdy, and the not-so-mainstream, like us.

Swarthmore is a Quaker school with a deep belief in peace and nonviolence. It is known for its rigorous curriculum and the lengthy reading lists that professors love to assign. I thoroughly enjoyed my first three years at the school, but once I hit my senior year, I was ready to get out there and work in the real world.

At another student group, the Committee in Support of the Palestinians and Lebanese, I met Anne-Marie Otey, a native New Yorker who would become a great friend of mine. The group was run by Jean-Louis Arcand, a Canadian student whose father had once served as Canada's ambassador to Lebanon.

Israel had invaded Lebanon in 1982, sending troops in as far north as Beirut. This triggered the Sabra and Shatila refugee camp massacre in September 1982 by the Lebanese Forces, a Christian militia in the Lebanese civil war, supported by the Israel Defense Forces. Several thousand Palestinians and Lebanese Shia were brutally killed. This atrocity left Arcand fuming. His hatred of the IDF scared me a little at the time but is something I now fully understand after the bloody Israeli invasion and bombing of Gaza, which started in October 2023. Walking out together after the meeting, through the halls of Parrish, I told Anne-Marie that I was gay. She smiled and said, "I know."

Anne-Marie also has parents of different religions. Her father is Catholic and her mother is Jewish. She studied at the renowned Stuyvesant High School in New York City, and lived in Bay Ridge, Brooklyn. She was a Lang Scholar at Swarthmore. We bonded over our love of fashion and politics. I fondly remember staying at her house and her mom enlisting me to sweep up the leaves in their backyard.

Although our hormones were certainly racing, there was surprisingly little sex happening at Swarthmore. Occasionally, a group of us would venture into nearby Philadelphia to visit the gay bars, where we danced, laughed, and soaked up the freedom those spaces offered. The college regularly funded student parties on campus, and we were fortunate to have a steady stream of distinguished academic and literary guests giving lectures. I remember Margaret Atwood coming once, and a concert by Suzanne Vega. We also started organizing an annual gay and lesbian film festival where we would find interesting documentaries and feature films to screen on campus.

12
SHORT SHORTS IN RIYADH

I first visited Saudi Arabia in 1969. Jamelah and I were dispatched from Geneva on a weekly flight to Jeddah on Saudi Arabian Airlines. Since we were flying solo, without an adult guardian, we had those little, plastic information pouches around our necks, signaling to ground and air staff that we needed special attention.

The flight from Geneva was on a Boeing 707, which soon became my favorite aircraft. In Jeddah, we connected to a domestic flight to Riyadh, where our grandmother Habiba lived. The plane was much smaller and had propellers. I don't remember much about this trip except the scary insects lurking in the stairwell between my grandmother's floor in the villa and where my uncle lived on the ground floor with his family.

The next trip I remember was in 1979, when we lived in Brazil. My dad and I flew on Royal Air Maroc from Brazil to Jeddah, with a layover and connecting flight in Casablanca. We flew first class, and the flight attendant had to suggest that I drink some juice after I had ordered one Coke too many.

I listened to Carol King's children's album *Really Rosie* on repeat with those rubber airline headphones that you stuck into your ears.

My father couldn't understand what Moroccans were saying in the country's commercial capital, so he resorted to speaking in classical Arabic, which sounded strange since it is usually reserved for the written word. But most people were able to understand him.

Running in the street had just become a health craze in the US with James Fixx's bestseller book "The Complete Book of Running". It was published in 1977, and I had a copy that I read cover to cover. This led me to run one day in the street in Riyadh, in my grandmother's neighborhood.

Riyadh was still the staunchly conservative heartland of Saudi Arabia, where my dad's older brother Abdulrahman had once screamed at my mother and sister to cover their faces when we were in a car with him. Its insularity still scared foreign diplomats, with many countries keeping their embassies in the cosmopolitan city of Jeddah well into the 1980s.

I still remember wearing red shorts and a white t-shirt as I jogged in Riyadh. A car pulled up alongside me and I stopped to see what the driver wanted. A Saudi man was at the wheel and asked me what I was doing. "I'm running to exercise myself," I replied.

"Your shorts are too short!", exclaimed the man. "You should cover your legs to the knee."

I didn't say anything and continued jogging as he drove away. Needless to say, this wasn't my last clash with the ultra-conservative mores of central Arabia.

13
A BEAUTIFUL VOICE FROM EGYPT TO MAKKAH

"I remember your grandfather's voice. It was beautiful. We used to listen to him when we lived in Makkah next to the Haram," said Faiza Ambah's grandmother to me in Arabic when I visited the Ambah home in Jeddah in the 1990s.

"You see! It's incredible she still remembers your grandfather's voice," Faiza said to me, smiling broadly.

Abdulzahir Abou-Alsamh was the name of my dad's father. He was born in Egypt in 1882 and died in 1951 in Paris on a stopover while traveling to the United States for treatment of kidney ailments.[1]

He was an imam and an Islamic scholar, who in 1926 went to Makkah to perform Haj. With him he had a letter from Rashid Rida, a leader of the Salafi movement in Egypt, addressed to King Abdulaziz al-Saud, saying he thought my grandfather would be a good candidate to be the imam of Masjid al-Haram in Makkah.[2]

---

1. Lauziere, Henri, *The Making of Salafism: Islamic Reform in the Twentieth Century*, (New York: Columbia University Press, 2016) pp. 73-77
2. Ibid

"The king immediately hired him and named him chief imam and *khatib* (one who delivers the sermon) at the holy mosque in Mecca. ...he also served as professor and supervisor of the faculty there. Abu al-Samh spent the rest of his life in Saudi Arabia but died on his way to the United States to receive treatment for kidney disease," writes Henri Lauziere in his book *"The Making of Salafism: Islamic Reform in the Twentieth Century"*.[3]

Scholars much later said that his appointment was perhaps a way to sidestep intense domestic jockeying for the prized position by appointing a foreigner to the post.

My grandfather's brother-in-law, Muhammad Abd al-Razzaq Hamza, who was the brother of my grandmother Habiba Hamza, was also given a letter of recommendation by Rida, and was later appointed the imam and *khatib* of the Prophet's Mosque in Madinah by Abdulaziz. He spent the rest of his life in Saudi Arabia until his death in Makkah in 1972.[4]

My father would tell me and Jamelah many stories about his father when we were growing up. He was a stern disciplinarian who believed that children should only be seen and not heard. If my dad and his brothers misbehaved as children, my grandfather would beat them. Despite this tough upbringing, I could tell that my father loved his father very much.

In the few photographs of my grandfather that I have seen, he looks like a tall and remarkable man, with piercing eyes and a white beard. It is a pity that he died before I was born. I would have liked to have known him.

He had three wives in total, with my grandmother being his second wife.

My father told us that they lived in a house right near the Haram, which until the expansion projects of the Holy Mosque started in the 1980s, was quite common. They lived without air-conditioning and

---

3. Ibid
4. Ibid

endured stifling heat in the summer. Many, including my family, would escape to Taif in the mountains or go to Cairo to escape the worst of the summer heat.

All of those old houses and buildings near the Haram are long gone now, having been torn down to make way for the expansion of the Holy Mosque. Today, a skyscraper containing a luxury hotel and a shopping mall sits adjacent to the mosque, in a scene my grandfather would be startled to see if he were still alive today.

14

THURSDAY NIGHTS AND BRIMAN JAIL

What did it mean to be gay in Saudi Arabia during the 1980s and 1990s? If one were overtly feminine and wore makeup and tight pants in public, there was the real risk of being stopped by the religious police, taken to one of their offices, and beaten until confessing to being a homosexual. The confession would lead to a quick sentence by a judge consisting of a jail term and flogging.

In 1990, I began dating a Filipino named Noel. He had a college degree and worked as an optometrist in an eyeglass shop.

I still remember the birthday cake Noel arranged for my celebration at our friend Aunty's house. It had fresh, yellow flowers decorating it, something I had never seen before.

He would sleep over at my apartment every Thursday night. I'd pick him up near his store at 10 p.m., just as he was closing. Thursday and Friday were still the weekend in Saudi. Many years later, it would be changed to Friday and Saturday to be more aligned with Western countries.

I was so in love with Noel that when I won a free trip for two to

London, I took him with me. We stayed with my friend from college Rob Luginbuhl, who was studying for his master's degree at the London School of Economics.

I drove Noel to my apartment on one of those Thursday night pickups. When we were parking near my building, I noticed a Saudi man following us in his car. He watched from his car as we walked into my building. I was freaked out, but Noel brushed it off. A few days later, I called his store to talk with Noel after not hearing from him. His colleagues told me that the *muttawas* (religious police) had arrested Noel! This sent chills through me.

"Are they going to come after me too?" I thought. I became paranoid after this, checking my rearview mirror every time I drove home from the newspaper, afraid that someone could be following me to arrest me for being gay.

After a few weeks I learned that Noel was being held in Briman jail. I found out which day was visiting day and went to see him. Arriving at the jail they asked for my ID and who I was visiting. I gave them Noel's name and passed through a metal detector. I was led into a courtyard that was attached to the main building. There was a fence on the side facing the building, where prisoners came out to speak to their visitors. I was shocked when I saw Noel. He looked gaunt and was dressed in a white prison uniform. We were around 10 feet apart and couldn't touch or hug each other.

He told me the *muttawa* had beaten the soles of his feet until he confessed. He had signed a "confession" in Arabic, just to make the beatings stop. The judge had sentenced him to nine months in prison and over 300 lashes.

I began visiting him weekly, giving him money to buy cigarettes and food while in jail. Then, I started the most improbable friendship in my life with Amin, the Coptic Egyptian "other" boyfriend of Noel. Noel had told me about him early in our relationship, and, being in love, I decided to accept it and continue dating him.

I first met Amin after he sent me a message saying he wanted to meet me to talk about Noel's predicament. I accepted, and we met for coffee at a local cafe. We quickly became friends, both of us subconsciously realizing that neither would end up with Noel.

Amin was an engineer who worked with one of the largest construction companies in Saudi Arabia. He lived in a pre-fab American-built house that looked like it was from the 1970s and had seen better days.

I eventually decided to travel to Manila to meet Noel's parents and siblings and tell them what had happened to their son and brother. Noel's father was a pastor at a conservative church, and Noel had never told his family that he was gay. Despite this, I'm sure that they knew in the back of their minds that he was gay.

Our meeting in their family home was awkward, but they received me well. Explaining to them what had happened was rather tricky, but I managed. They thanked me for coming to Manila and for visiting Noel in jail.

They looked stunned and worried. It seemed like I had just told them that Noel had passed away.

When I used their bathroom, after they had offered me soft drinks and some snacks, I marveled at the modest but tidy house that Noel had grown up in, and couldn't help feeling sad for being the messenger of such bad news.

Later, on my way back to Saudi Arabia, I cried on the plane, thinking of Noel in jail.

Back in Jeddah, I decided to fly to Washington, DC, to see if I could rally some support for Noel on Capitol Hill. I managed to meet with a congressman, but he told me he could do nothing, as Noel was not a U.S. citizen.

Feeling crushed and defeated, I remember crying all the way back to Jeddah on my flight from Paris to Saudi. I had reached the lowest point in the Saudi chapter of my life. After serving his sentence and being flogged, Noel was deported back to Manila. He stayed there for about a year before moving to Los Angeles and finding a job as an optometrist.

In 2001, I visited and stayed with Noel in his Hollywood apartment. We watched TV together at night when he came home from work, and once we went to see a movie together. But nothing sexual happened between us. The horror of what had happened to Noel was still in our minds, something neither of us will ever forget.

Amin and I continue as friends.

15
FROM JEDDAH TO QUEZON CITY

Before living and working in Jeddah, I never dreamed I would become so involved with the Philippines, its people, and culture. Until the late 1980s, the only Filipinos I knew or had heard of were Pilar, the Philippine wife of an American neighbor of ours in Geneva, and the Marcoses. I still remember her showing my mother and I the large scar she had on her hand from when, as a child, she tried to escape from a Japanese internment camp in the Philippines during World War II. She cut herself badly on the thick barbed wire that encircled their camp.

The other infamous Filipinos I had heard of were Ferdinand and Imelda Marcos, the power couple who ruled the Philippines from 1966 until the People's Power Revolution of 1986.

But it was at *Arab News*, when I was first assigned to edit the Features section, that I would meet the first Filipino to become a good friend of mine.

One day in 1989, a Filipino named Narciso Chan dropped by our office and struck up a conversation with me. He was working for Stallion Records, a newly formed music company in Jeddah that was releasing licensed BMG Music CDs in the Kingdom. Ciso wanted coverage for his releases in *Arab News*. We quickly became friends, and he was pivotal in introducing me to the wider Filipino community in Jeddah.

My first visit to Manila was in 1991 when I was sent on a press trip to Taiwan. I was able to route my return through Manila, where I stayed with my friend Nestor at his house in Quezon City. I instantly felt at home in the friendly chaos of the Philippine capital.

Epic traffic jams and flooded streets when super typhoons hit the islands, were all part and parcel of living in Manila. But it was the legendary friendliness of Filipinos, especially with foreigners, that made me fall in love with the country, its food, culture and its people. A recent online comparison between Manila, Bangkok and Jakarta, comparing their infrastructure and friendliness to tourists, ranked Manila first in friendliness, while it lost out to Bangkok in terms of shopping facilities.

I returned in 1992 to cover the presidential elections in which Fidel Ramos, a former general, was elected president. This time I stayed at the family home of my best friend Aris Anonas in Santa Ana. His father and sister soon took to liking me, and I felt totally embraced by my new "family". I filed a story every few days for two weeks. I had to fax my stories to Jeddah. Ciso generously allowed me to use his office fax for this. Several of my stories made the front page of *Arab News*.

The star of this election campaign wasn't retired military leader Ramos but the delightfully quirky Miriam Defensor Santiago, who was a fast-talking lawyer from Iloilo. She had been appointed as Secretary of Agrarian Reform in the government of Cory Aquino. She lost the election to Ramos but would go on to be elected twice to the Philippine Senate. She was also the first Asian woman from a developing country to be elected a judge at the International Criminal Court.

Known for her fast chattering in English, Santiago was known for zingy comebacks to other politicians during debates and speeches. She was a brilliant woman who sadly died in 2016 from lung cancer.

Julie Javellana, a local journalist, helped me while I was in Manila, and she would become *Arab News'* correspondent in the Philippines. I had met her husband Sammy Santos when he was working in Jeddah as a reporter for *Saudi Gazette*. He introduced me to Julie when I went on that first of many reporting trips to the Philippines. She and her husband became close friends of mine whom I always saw when I was in town.

Sammy loved drinking beer, and on one of my trips to Manila took me to the rather infamous Hobbit House bar which was entirely staffed by little people. There we sat, drank beer and talked for hours. Luckily, we took a taxi home, as neither of us was capable of safely driving a car.

A few years later, I interviewed former president Corazon Aquino, who had been out of office for a long time. I found her very formal and cold. Unlike the Marcoses, she was very low-key, dressed in modest clothes, and was known for her devotion to the Catholic Church.

Perhaps it was because of the tragedy of having her husband Sen. Ninoy Aquino assassinated on the tarmac of Manila International Airport when he came back from exile on Aug. 21, 1983. She never seemed quite the same after that.

But I became a fan of her daughter Kris Aquino, a wildly famous actress and television host. I loved her slight American accent when speaking Tagalog, and her effervescent personality was fun to watch. For years I would watch her on ABS-CBN in Jeddah via satellite. Sadly, Kris began having serious health problems and left showbiz many years ago.

16

MACHO DANCERS AND MASSAGE PARLORS

In Manila, as in many cities touched and shaped by a colonial past and an uncertain modernity, the nights revealed something more honest than the days. One could not say one had truly seen the city without a visit to its gay bars, thinly veiled theatres of masculine performance, and to one of its many massage parlors. These places, while peripheral in geography and repute, held a central place in the social life of a certain kind of Filipino man and his foreign guests.

The dancers in these clubs were called macho dancers. The name itself was a fiction, an attempt at dignity perhaps, or a concession to desire—both the dancers' and their clientele's. They were supposed to be straight, or at the very least straight-acting, though nobody believed it. But the illusion was everything. There was a notion, perhaps born of American films or local church hypocrisy, that gay men desired only the masculine, the unyielding, the uninterested. The men on stage were meant to embody this idea: muscular, aloof, waving their erect penises in the faces of cheering spectators—some older men, quietly desperate.

In Quezon City, home to the University of the Philippines, the best gay clubs could be found. I had gone to one called US Male with friends in 2000. The memory is blurred, more from the weight of time than alcohol. The club had an elevated runway. The men walked down one by one, illuminated by warm, theatrical light. They performed not so much for our approval as for our money. To many, it was a dream fulfilled. To me, it was fantasy come true.

It was through Aris, a friend with a knowing eye, that I came to the Phoenix Massage Parlor. It was in a modest, gray house—where men, stripped of pretense but not hope, stood in a line for selection. The manager, a man who had long since ceased to believe in what he said, would recite a brief biography for each: their charm, their strength, their supposed kindness. It was a kind of human résumé, spoken aloud under harsh fluorescent light. But the truth of the experience—whether pleasure or disappointment—lay upstairs, in dimly lit rooms with narrow beds and thin towels. The massages were adequate. The endings, happy or not, depended on one's generosity and expectations.

There had been, years earlier, a film about such men. *Macho Dancer*, directed by Lino Brocka. It told the story of a provincial boy abandoned by an American lover. What followed was predictable: the descent into Manila's seedy clubs, the struggle to survive, the betrayal of ideals. The film was hacked to pieces by the censors, shocked by its honesty. Yet a copy made its way to the Toronto Film Festival, and there, far from the heat and shame of the islands, it was applauded.

Brocka died relatively young, in a car crash in Quezon City, at 52. A great filmmaker, he was a chronicler of truth in a country that rarely wanted to see it.

17

OVERSEAS WORKERS AND THE ARAB WORLD

The Philippines had long ago accepted its condition: a nation exporting people rather than goods. Since the 1980s, its most reliable product had been its labor—Filipino men and women working abroad as nurses, shop clerks, engineers, housemaids. This, too, fed the gay bars of Manila. The supply of youthful, underpaid men seemed endless.

Among the hardest lands to work in were the Arab countries, where the wealth was new, the rules rigid, and the justice elusive. Many Filipino workers, once in the Gulf, found their passports taken, their hours long, their wages uncertain. Some were never paid. They lived in limbo, betwixt contract and betrayal.

One of the problematic employers was the construction behemoth Saudi Binladen Group, founded by Muhammad bin Laden, a Yemeni who had arrived in Saudi Arabia a poor man in 1931. He built roads, then palaces. He knew the royal family. He was given the honor of building the kingdom's mosques. At one time, he even oversaw the maintenance of the Al-Aqsa Mosque in Jerusalem.

He died in 1967. His sons took over. The company grew fat on government contracts to expand the holy cities—Makkah and Madinah. Money flowed. But not always to the workers. My friend Amin, an Egyptian engineer who worked at Binladin, told me of months without salary, of debts piling up. He only survived by using credit cards. The company had the funds. But the Saudi government often delayed payment, and the contractors, in turn, delayed their obligations to the men who built their monuments.

Language, religion, pride—these made life harder for Asian workers. Many Arabs believed themselves superior to their Asian employees. It was not openly spoken but understood. And yet, Filipinos adapted. They learned Arabic quickly, smiled when necessary, rarely complained. They became indispensable. Loyal. Hardworking. They sang during breaks, mended their uniforms, accepted the indignities with stoicism. This was what made them beloved by their employers, even as they were underpaid.

There were worse stories. One that circulated involved a Filipino shepherd in Saudi Arabia. He was tasked with tending goats in the countryside while his employer lived comfortably in the city. For years, the man received no salary. He waited, believing promises. Eventually, a team from the Philippine embassy rescued him. A labor court forced the employer to pay. The man went home. No one knows what became of him.

By contrast, the Saudi workforce itself was often idle. Civil servants, once hired, could not be dismissed. Productivity was low. Some local workers were accused of wasting time at work by drinking endless cups of tea, and taking time off when a relative had supposedly died. They weren't the most efficient workers in the world. To combat the preference of the private sector for foreign workers, the government introduced Saudization in the 1980s, setting quotas for local hires. Employers resisted. They preferred the foreign workers—cheaper, more compliant, easier to dismiss. They said a Saudi cost three times more than an Indian or Filipino, and worked less.

Youth unemployment among Saudi men hovered around thirty percent in those years. For women, it was worse. Educated, but largely excluded, they stayed home. Most eventually married and followed tradition.

Now, all that is changing. Muhammad bin Salman—the Crown Prince, the reformer— has upended the old order. Women now work in shops, at airports, in government offices. They drive cars. They no longer need to cover their hair. It is not revolution, but it feels like one. Today, it is common to be welcomed into the Kingdom by a female passport officer at the airport. Even Uber has women drivers.

These changes, however real, feel sudden. Only a few years ago, women could not work in retail. Their work world was limited to jobs in medicine and education. They were visible yet unseen. The 2018 decree that allowed them to drive was spoken of in hushed tones, as if it had dropped from heaven, unexplained.

The world changes. But beneath the surface, the old habits persist: the commodification of bodies in Manila, the silent labor of Filipinos in faraway deserts, the inequality masked by smiles and salary slips. Some stories are told. Others remain behind closed doors. But all are part of the same narrative—the longing for dignity in places that offer very little of it.

18

MANILA MOODS

In 1993 *Arab News* decided to dedicate whole news pages to specific regions of the world, to aggregate news for our Filipino, Indian, Pakistani and Western readers.

Therefore, we started daily Philippine, India, Pakistan and Americas news pages. Our managing editor Haider Kazim approached me one day and asked me if I would like to write a weekly opinion column for the Philippines page. I said "yes" and that is how *Manila Moods* was born.

In the column I wrote about Philippine politics, Overseas Filipino Workers, their plight in the Gulf, and about popular culture in general. There was no scarcity of stories of OFWs being abused by violent employers in Saudi, Kuwait and the UAE. Domestic workers were especially vulnerable as they were mostly women and lived in their employers' homes. Many Gulf employers treated their maids as indentured servants, making them work extremely long hours, confiscating their passports, and not allowing them days off.

A few of the male employers sexually abused the maids, which would bring violent reprisals against the maids from the wives of the abusers. A particularly gruesome case was a Kuwaiti couple who had employed a Filipino maid, whom they beat regularly and in a final act of barbarity had killed her and chopped her body up. When the police raided their home, they found pieces of the maid in the couples' deep freezer.

But Gulf employers were hardly the only ones who mistreated Filipio workers. Some affluent Lebanese families who employed female Filipinos as maids and nannies, fled their homes in the mountains during one of the regular flare-ups of fighting between the different sects in Lebanon, and left behind their maids in their homes, often locking them in, unwilling to take them along or send them back to the Philippines. Harrowing stories of abandoned workers soon surfaced, causing the Philippines to impose a ban on the export of workers to Lebanon.

This was a frequent action that Manila used against countries that were especially bad in their treatment of OFWs, but the sheer economic push of poor Filipinos wanting to work abroad and send dollars home, would soon overturn these bans.

I felt an affinity to the suffering of foreign workers in the Kingdom, since I too was half-foreign and had not grown up in Saudi Arabia. My white skin and green eyes, that I inherited from my American mother, made me stand out in this Arab country. Most people, both foreigners and Saudis, upon meeting me thought I was American or Lebanese. I had to explain to them my origins, and even then some Saudis couldn't believe that I was Saudi.

My column generated a lot of controversy and attention. One time I was flying to Manila from Jeddah, and a Filipino passenger on the same flight sneered at me and said, "I know you don't like President Joseph Estrada!" I shrugged my shoulders.

Estrada was a huge movie star in the Philippines and was elected president in 1998. He served until 2001, when the Supreme Court ousted him. I had written many columns criticizing his performance as president.

Another time, President Ramos was visiting Jeddah and had a town hall meeting scheduled with the local Filipino community. I went to cover the event for my column, but the organizers initially refused to let me in, claiming it was only for the Filipino community.

"I'm a journalist covering this event for *Arab News*. I have the right to attend!" I argued at the entrance. After waiting for another 15 minutes, they finally relented and let me in.

I would continue writing *Manila Moods* for another 14 years until 2007.

Many years later I would learn that my father had complained to my American cousin Laura about my column. "Why is Rasheed writing about the Filipinos?" he asked her, barely hiding his contempt of the idea.

19
CHRISTIAN SCIENCE MONITOR AND THE WASHINGTON TIMES

Working under the strict censorship in the Kingdom, I became increasingly frustrated by such restrictions. That is when I began writing for the *Christian Science Monitor* as a correspondent, while continuing my job at *Arab News*.

I got this job thanks to my dear friend Faiza Ambah, who worked with me at *Arab News*. She had been the Monitor's correspondent in Saudi Arabia and had now moved on to be the *Washington Post's* correspondent.

The story that got the most attention was one I wrote about Saudi women who blogged and challenged societal norms by criticizing social and religious aspects of Saudi society. American readers loved my story as it gave them insights into what was then a rather closed-off country.

I also started writing for the *Al-Ahram Weekly*, a publication of the esteemed *Al-Ahram* Arabic newspaper in Cairo.

In 2002, I started writing for the *Washington Times,* a conservative daily newspaper owned by the Moonies. My friend Michael was appalled, but I saw it as a way of reaching different types of readers in Washington, including President George W. Bush, whom I knew read the paper regularly. Today, several decades later, I'm not sure that I would write again for the *Washington Times* given how polarized we have become in America.

I wrote about the Saudi reform activists who had been arrested by the government and imprisoned for asking for freedom of expression and a constitutional monarchy. Saudi Arabia was and still is an absolute monarchy run by the Al-Saud royal family since the founding of the Kingdom in 1932.

The activists were eventually put on trial in Riyadh, the country's capital. I flew there to cover the trial for the *Washington Times*, but none of the reporters or family members of the accused were allowed into the court building. So, we all stood outside in the parking lot in front of the courthouse, waiting for any news from the lawyers inside.

As the afternoon drew to a close, the nearby mosques began calling for the Maghreb prayers. None of us wanted to pray, so we stayed in the parking lot. But the religious police showed up and started shouting at us to go to the nearest mosque to pray.

We ended up running down narrow side streets to escape from the mutawwas' admonitions. As expected, the activists were found guilty of working against the ruler. They were sentenced to 10 years in jail. They were eventually released when King Abdullah pardoned them.

20

MOVING TO MANILA

I landed in Manila in December 2000 with my two cats, Negra and Pinay, and my Saluki dog. The immigration officers did not bat an eyelash when I handed them my American passport, apparently finding it normal that a tourist was entering their country with such a large entourage. Americans and Saudis can enter the Philippines visa-free for 90 days, so that's what I did.

I cannot remember who gave me the Saluki, but he was beautiful, and I wasn't going to leave him behind in Jeddah.

"You are going to have to pay a fee to bring these animals into the country," said a Customs officer. I knew that in advance, and I had gotten all the medical clearances to export my pets from Saudi Arabia and import them into the Philippines.

My reason for suddenly moving to the Philippines was my boyfriend, Ronald. We had been together since 1992, when a gay friend of mine had introduced me to him.

Ronald worked at a Bin Dawood supermarket and grew up poor outside Manila. He was around 5'9", tall for a Filipino, had a mustache, and was goodlooking. He was always smiling and joking around.

After a few years of dating, he resigned from the supermarket, went home to Manila, and after a few months came back on a work visa I managed to get from a prince who was selling visas on the black market.

Ronald became my stay-at-home husband, cleaning our house and clothes, and preparing our meals, while I went to work every day at the newspaper. I subscribed to the Filipino TV channel TFC, which we got in Jeddah via satellite, as I thought this would help diminish some of Ronald's homesickness. I watched it almost as much as he did to keep up with the political news and showbiz scandals I wrote about in my *Manila Moods* column.

Ronald and I were quickly accepted as a couple in the Filipino community, and we often went to parties together. One weekend in 1997, we were invited to the birthday party of a gay acquaintance in the Ruwais district. The district was a working-class neighborhood, with a mixture of Yemeni, Egyptian and Filipino residents.

We thought about going, but later decided we just wanted to stay home and watch a movie. As it turned out, our guardian angels were working overtime for us! The main attraction of the party was drag performances. Unfortunately for all who attended, a disgruntled former friend of the celebrant decided to screw-over everyone in attendance by calling the religious police and telling them about the party and its location.

The raid on the party happened as the performers were in full act, lip-synching furiously to such gay anthems as "It's Raining Men", and wearing makeup, wigs, and women's clothes. They could hardly deny that they were gay. All were herded onto a bus and taken to a police station and duly booked for being homosexual and wearing women's clothes. It is against the law in Saudi Arabia to cross-dress, and also to be gay.

Many of my friends were arrested and sentenced from seven to nine months' jail time and lashings. The arrests were shocking as we thought that as long as we did not act too outrageously in public and had understanding neighbors, we could get away with these parties.

"What if I had been arrested? What would I say to my Saudi relatives and parents?!" I kept thinking. Two of my friends were among those arrested. Kuki, a barber, who is now successfully running his family-owned gas station in Candon, Illocos, and who never went back to the Gulf, and Bambi, an executive assistant now retired in Manila.

The shame probably would have caused much drama and lashing out at me for being gay and mixing with the "clearly inferior" foreign gays. My father had many times told me and Jamelah that in Islam, it is expected that anyone doing something sinful should do so in private and not talk about it in public. Flaunting the immoral behavior in public could encourage others to commit similar acts. It is the Muslim version of the US military's "Don't ask, don't tell" policy adopted by President Bill Clinton for gay military personnel.

21
MOONSHINE AND 9/11

Apart from my Filipino gay friends, I also had several Western gay and straight friends in Jeddah. With Saudi Arabia not being an extremely family-friendly country because of all the restrictions on women, many gay men were hired to work there.

Most of these friends were British and Irish. Hugh worked as an English-language teacher at a Saudi college; Tony likewise, and Alan was an interior designer who decorated the palaces of Saudi princes and rich businessmen. All drank heavily, and their drink of choice, given that alcohol was banned in the country, was the locally distilled "Sidiki", a clear and potent drink. "Sidiki" means "my friend" in Arabic, and that is how everyone referred to the local moonshine. It was secretly sold in 1.5-liter mineral water bottles. To find some you needed to have a connection who knew a good source of the drink. Drinkers kept their Sidiki suppliers a closely guarded secret, only telling their closest friends about them.

Danjean, a Filipina woman who lived in the building next to mine, was one such connection. Ronald had introduced me to her years earlier at a party. Her husband distilled the spirit in their apartment, and she took care of sales.

But the stream of people coming empty-handed to their apartment, then leaving with bottles of sid (as it is colloquially shortened to) in shopping bags soon became much too obvious for the authorities to ignore. So, one day when I was returning to my apartment, I saw police and religious police cars outside their building, and I knew their jig was up. I had just been over to their house a few days earlier and thanked my lucky stars that I had escaped being arrested. Danjean managed to escape arrest by hiding in a neighboring apartment, but her husband wasn't so lucky and was arrested and served a jail term before being deported back to the Philippines.

Sid needed to be mixed with tonic water or fruit juices to be drunk. You could have a sid and Coke or a sid and Seven-Up. This stuff was potent! Drinking too much, too quickly, invariably led to throwing up and a massive hangover the next day.

Those wishing to have a lighter alcoholic drink were in luck, as many expats made homemade white and red wine. They would buy large quantities of grape juice at the supermarkets, and with sugar and yeast, ferment the juice and then bottle it. This was especially true in the housing compounds favored by Western expats. I had a Dutch friend, Martina, married to an American, who regularly had me over for white wine spritzers as we sat around their pool.

Martina was an excellent watercolor artist. I had met her for the first time at an exhibition of my Uncle Anas, who was an avid amateur photographer. He introduced me to her, and we fast became good friends.

Another friend was Lee, an Australian journalist married to an American pilot of Saudi Arabian Airlines. They lived in the huge Saudia compound and had a tiki-bar in their living room, which they used regularly during the parties they threw.

Lee worked as a radio announcer at Jeddah Radio, which was run by the Ministry of Information. She did a sort-of Desert Island Discs program in which she interviewed interesting people and played music tracks chosen by the guests. I was invited as a guest, and I gave her my tape of Rickie Lee Jones' 1979 song "Chuck-E's in Love".

"It doesn't have anything iffy in it," she asked me, explaining that she had to run it by the station's censors to check for any naughty or forbidden words in the lyrics.

"No, there isn't," I replied. And it passed, as I knew it would.

Lee had shoulder-length blond hair worn a la Farrah Fawcett and had skin so tanned that she sometimes looked leathery. She was from Queensland, the Gold Coast near the Great Barrier Reef, and loved the beach. She was quite athletic.

Lee was also our restaurant reviewer at *Arab News*, and I soon became in charge of editing her column and placing it and accompanying photos on the Feature page. "Gourmet Gossip" was the cheeky name given to it. As the paper didn't have a budget to pay for the food she reviewed, Lee depended on the goodwill of restaurants to provide her with free meals in return for a write-up in the paper. I wasn't a fan of this set-up, as it clearly influenced her opinions. But she was very professional and never gushed in her column. I soon became a frequent guest at her review meals and loved the delicious and varied food we ate.

My Western gay friends were obsessed with Arab and Pakistani men. Some of them forged long-term relationships with these boyfriends, but were always treated as side pieces, the men they liked invariably married and ostensibly straight. That perceived manliness is what they procured, laughing off white, gay Westerners as repellant and limp wristed.

"God, I don't want to be in love with anyone!" exclaimed Terry to me once. "I can't stand those Western poofters."

Terry was Australian and worked with me at the paper. He was raucous and always cracking jokes. I liked him a lot. He was rather manic but was an excellent writer and editor. I spent many an evening at his house having drinks with our friends and chatting.

Leo was another British friend who loved Pakistani men. He would regularly go cruising and pick up rough trade. He also worked as an editor at the paper with me and would show up a few times with a black eye and a fantastical story of how a trick had hit him while stealing his TV and money.

"It was horrible!" Leo would tell me, a slight smile on his lips. I could tell he got a sexual frisson from the rough trade. But I worried that one day he might lose more than just a few material possessions.

Leo was very generous and one of the kindest persons I have ever met in my life. We often went out together to eat, or he would invite me over to his apartment. I even met his mother when Leo managed to get her a visit visa and she came to Jeddah and stayed for a month. After a few years he left *Arab News* for a job teaching English at the British Council in Lahore, Pakistan. But then 9/11 struck, and he was evacuated to Britain as a security precaution.

One Western gay man that wasn't my friend was John Bradley. He was tall, thin, white and had a bald head. He was born in 1970 and had grown up working class in a housing estate in England. He was hired to work at *Arab News* in 2001 as an editor. He had previously worked as a copy editor at *Al-Ahram Weekly* in Cairo, Egypt. An Egyptian colleague of mine at the paper had worked with John in Cairo and recommended that we hire him.

What a mistake that was! John was abrasive and hated anything American. On 9/11, we were all in the newsroom at *Arab News* working and then we started watching CNN on the TV monitors we had hanging from the ceiling, as reports started coming in that a plane had hit one of the towers of the World Trade Center in New York.

"I think a small plane hit the building," I said to a colleague, as we watched the initial images. But we soon found out that it had been a much larger commercial jet that had slammed into the tower. It was only when the second jet hit the other tower did it click that this was a coordinated attack on New York.

"Those American imperialists deserve these attacks after all the

Arabs they've killed in the Middle East," spat out John, grinning rather maniacally.

I was shocked. I could understand Arab resentment against America's support of Israel and of Arab dictators. But flying jets filled with innocent civilians into buildings? That was another story altogether.

I eventually became aware that John was gay, after overhearing him telling other gay staff members that he liked young boys. He even offered a DVD of kiddie porn to my gay Saudi colleague, who declined the offer.

"I like to live in working class areas. There I find a lot of willing young boys that I give small gifts and money to in return for sex," John once told me and several other gay friends.

This pedophilia would soon catch up with him. On a trip to Singapore to visit his Singaporean boyfriend, John was called from Jeddah by a friend, who warned him not to come back to the kingdom. The police were looking for him, after parents of boys he had diddled with complained to the authorities.

And just like that, John resigned by email and flew back to the UK. He had his friends in Jeddah sell his car and belongings.

In 2005, we found out why John had wanted so badly to work at *Arab News*. His incendiary book "Saudi Arabia Exposed: Inside a Kingdom in Crisis" was published, and in it he unleashed all of his venom against Saudi Arabia and the royal family. It was widely reviewed, and John was invited to some talk shows to discuss his book. In it he claimed to have been the only Western journalist based full-time in the kingdom, as he was researching his book. He also claimed he spoke fluent Arabic, which he had learned in Cairo.

John then wrote a book on Egypt, later claiming that he had correctly predicted the Arab Spring revolution that overthrew longtime dictator Hosni Mubarak. Starting in 2011, he also had a regular writing stint at the rightwing *Spectator* magazine in London, writing more incendiary copy on Saudi Arabia.

Then he disappeared and literally fell off the map. He had

announced on his website that he was going to stop writing because of some serious health issues he was undergoing. John was famously private, so his disappearance didn't cause much alarm.

And then suddenly in the Feb. 15, 2025, issue of the *Spectator*, its executive editor Laura Prendergast, wrote a piece entitled: "The Mysterious Life of John R. Bradley". In it she revealed that John had moved to Mexico in early 2020 and was living there with two dogs in a small house near Guadalajara.

He had cut off all communication with the magazine and with his brother back in England. His neighbors in Mexico said he was very reserved, staying in his house most of the time, and did not mix with the locals. Then one day the neighbors complained of a foul smell coming from John's house. They contacted the police who broke down the front door and found John dead in his locked bathroom. His dogs were alive in another room. He had been dead for at least eight days.

No one seems to know if the Mexican police ordered an autopsy, or what happened to John's body. Was he cremated? Or was he buried as an indigent? *The Spectator* didn't know.

John had allegedly contracted dengue fever while in Mexico, a disease spread by mosquitos, which causes fever, body aches, and can cause swelling of the heart. So, had he died of complications from that? Had a trick he brought home killed him? Or did the Saudis order a hit on him as revenge for the anti-Saudi venom he had spewed?

These questions are probably never going to be completely answered, but it was a sad fate even for someone as hateful as John. He was 50 when he died.

22

MUNICIPAL ELECTIONS THAT LED NOWHERE

I never thought that I would witness elections in Saudi Arabia, let alone that I would participate in them. But that is exactly what happened when I voted in the municipal elections in 2005, the first in the kingdom since the 1960s.

Following the 9/11 attacks, in which 15 of the 19 plane hijackers were Saudi, US President George W. Bush started a campaign of trying to bring democracy to Saudi Arabia. The theory was that if the kingdom were semi-democratic, elections would serve as an escape valve for the population's grievances.

Saudi Arabia had experimented with municipal elections as early as the 1920s, when King Abdulaziz ibn Saud approved them for Jeddah, Makkah, Madinah and Taif in the Hejaz region. It was an effort to establish loyal local governments for these cities after Abdulaziz's forces wrested control of Hejaz from Ottoman and Hashemite rulers. Later, King Saud ibn Abdulaziz ordered more municipal elections between 1954 and 1962. After Saud's abdication in 1964, King Faisal ibn Abdulaziz and further kings did not hold municipal elections.

In 2005, the kingdom announced that it would hold municipal

elections for cities across the country. Half of the council members would be appointed by the government, while the other half would be elected. All the members would be male.

I remember registering for the elections and being issued a government voting ID with my picture. The whole country was abuzz with what was seen as a stab at democracy, and that was exciting. Candidates handed out fliers at campaign tents that they pitched at various areas in Jeddah. Their platforms varied, but with the limitations that municipal councils had to begin with, they couldn't promise too much to voters. Saudi Arabia's rulers concentrate power in the capital Riyadh, allowing very little autonomy at the local level.

On the appointed day I went to the polls and voted. I was feeling rather detached about the whole exercise, having voted in the U.S. when I was in college. Somewhere in the back of my mind I knew this exercise was the Saudi government going through the motions of trying to pretend that it cared about democracy, in a bid to please President Bush and the U.S. government. But I also knew that true democracy was not something the Saudi royal family would ever seriously contemplate. They had always used the argument that if Saudis were allowed to freely elect their leaders, very conservative candidates would win. And that was what happened with many of the candidates that were elected.

But some candidates found unique platforms to campaign on. One was a businessman in Riyadh who wanted to vastly cut back on the number of foreign drivers that worked in the country. Since women were still not allowed to drive yet, most Saudi families that could afford it would hire a foreign driver, mainly from Indonesia and Pakistan, to drive the females in the family around. This created a large influx of foreign men who lived with the families they worked for. One only had to go to a shopping mall in the evening to see the foreign drivers sitting together at the entrances, while their female bosses shopped inside.

I flew to Riyadh to interview the candidate for a newspaper story

I was working on. He invited me to come along with him on an evening drive. Our conversation was constantly being interrupted by phone calls from outraged voters, which he played on the car's speakers so that I could hear them. They were furious that he was trying to get rid of the drivers that kept the women in their families mobile and able to go to school, shopping, jobs and doctor's appointments on their own. Without the drivers, the fathers, brothers and sons of these women would be forced to ferry their female relatives around.

Needless to say, that candidate did not win a seat on the Riyadh municipal council. Further elections were held in 2011 and 2015, with women only being allowed to vote and be candidates in the 2015 polls. New elections should have been held in 2019, but the Coronavirus pandemic struck in March 2020, and the kingdom endured a tough shutdown. All talk of elections vanished overnight, and the general population did not seem too upset by this setback.

23

SAUDI ARABIA A QUASI-AMERICAN POSSESSION

Saudi Arabia has always been a quasi-American possession ever since Standard Oil of California struck oil in Dammam on March 3, 1938. The country may have been insular, extremely conservative and wary of foreigners in the central Qur'an belt, but the immense wealth that oil brought to the kingdom, inexorably tied the fate of this nation to the United States.

The Kingdom of Saudi Arabia was unified in 1932 after a long campaign by King Abdulaziz al-Saud and his Wahabi allies to conquer and subjugate disparate regions around the Arabian Peninsula. Arguably, the most difficult to subdue was the Kingdom of Hejaz on the Red Sea coast, which included the holy cities of Madinah and Makkah, and the port of Jeddah. It had been part of the Ottoman Empire, but with the defeat of the Ottomans in 1916, became a kingdom ruled by the Hashemites. But they did not last long, being conquered by the forces of King Abdulaziz after the British switched their support to the Al-Sauds in 1924, and supplied them with machine guns that other fighting forces did not have access to.

The vast desert of the Rub-Al Khali (the Empty Quarter), and the harsh temperatures had never made this part of the peninsula attractive to the British imperialists, who preferred to control the coastal areas of what are now Iraq, Kuwait, Bahrain, Qatar, the United Arab Emirates, Oman and Yemen, which is all the way on the other side of the peninsula.

The Americans were locked out of the oil fields of Iraq by the British and French through the 1920 San Remo Petroleum Agreement, so after oil shortages during World War I, the U.S. decided it needed to find alternative sources of oil in the region.

SoCal had initially been unsuccessful in finding any oil fields in Saudi Arabia, so it sold a 50 percent share in its subsidiary, California-Arabian Standard Oil, to the Texas Oil Company (Texaco) in 1936.

Drilling its seventh Dammam well was when Americans finally hit oil, naming the well Dammam No. 7. This well began producing 1,500 barrels a day and gave hope to the company that they would find more. In 1944, its name was changed to Arabian American Oil Co. (Aramco), and in 1948 Standard Oil of New Jersey (later known as Exxon) bought a 30 percent stake in Aramco, and Socony Vacuum (later known as Exxon) bought 10 percent of the company. SoCal and Texaco's shares of Aramco were reduced to 30 percent each respectively.

But the arrival of the white, Christian Americans was a shock to the local Saudi population in the Eastern region of Saudi Arabia. The country was still poor and undeveloped. The Saudi writer Abdul Rahman Munif wrote movingly about the displacement of local populations that lived near or on oil fields in his multi-volume novel "Cities of Salt", published in Beirut in 1984. Munif was stripped of his Saudi citizenship for writing critically of the royal family and the country. He ended up living and working most of his life for oil entities in Syria and Iraq.

Aramco built a very large housing and office compound for all its American employees and their families in Dhahran, the twin city of Dammam. It had streets of what looked like typical American suburban homes, with lush, imported grass lawns. Women were allowed to drive in the compound, something Saudi women would only obtain the right to do more than 70 years later in 2018.

Supermarkets in the compound had imported American goods. There was a cinema showing the latest Hollywood movies, and Aramco even had its own television station, which began broadcasting in September 1957. It was the second TV station in the Middle East, after Iraqi TV, and initially only had one hour of daily programming. By the 1960s and 1970s it broadcast many American TV series dubbed into Arabic, such as "Perry Mason", and was eagerly watched by Saudis who lived in the region. It devoted one-third of its programming to educational shows.

Its last transmission was in December 1998, closing down in part because of the anger of some Saudi viewers that its shows were not censored. By then Saudi state television had two channels on the air, one in Arabic and the other in English.

Aramco was so important to the American economy that Trans World Airlines flew regularly to Dhahran from New York, the plane stopping in Paris and Cairo on the way. These flights started in the 1946 and lasted until TWA's demise in 2001. TWA was also hired in 1946 to help establish and run the national airline, Saudi Arabian Airlines. Its management contract was for five years.

Dhahran International Airport's magnificent new terminal was inaugurated in 1962 and was designed by the Japanese American architect Minoru Yamasaki, using elements of Islamic architecture in a modern fashion. It has beautiful tall arches and a control tower that looks like a minaret. It was built on what had been a US airfield, used during World War II. This airport was renamed King Abdul Aziz Air Base, after a new international airport was built in Dammam in 1999.

My mother first stepped on Saudi soil in 1963 after arriving on a TWA flight from New York to Dhahran.

"I remember that I was taken to the Aramco compound to spend the night before my domestic flight to Riyadh," my mother told me.

"I was pleasantly surprised when I found iceberg lettuce in my dinner at Aramco," she reminisced.

Pan American Airlines later flew nonstop in the 1980s from Dhahran to New York using its 747-Special Performance planes for the 13-hour flight.

24
SHABU AND A RADICAL DEPARTURE

In the late 1990s, there was a boom in crystal meth usage in the Philippines, where it was relatively cheap, produced in labs, and highly addictive. Drug syndicates from mainland China were accused of importing meth to the Philippines and spreading it on the streets. Soon enough, some Filipinos imported the drug to Saudi Arabia, despite the kingdom having a strict death penalty policy for drug carriers.

Endless notices in the Saudi press of Pakistanis being executed for trying to smuggle heroin into the country were an indication of the demand for these drugs and the deep poverty that drove some Pakistanis to try to smuggle heroin into the country, usually in balloons that they swallowed after being promised a payout if successful. Of course, this meant that only the poor smugglers were being killed, and not the drug lords themselves.

On a trip once coming back from Pakistan, a Saudi Customs agent at Jeddah airport pulled me aside and motioned me to step into a room where he was going to frisk me for drugs. When I flashed my Saudi passport at him, he apologized and smiled at me, ushering me out of the room. Apparently, all non-Saudi passengers arriving from Pakistan were viewed as potential smugglers.

In the Philippines, crystal meth was commonly called "shabu" and could easily be found in any big city. Users reported feeling a surge of happiness, and bouts of energy that would cause them to perform several tasks in a row without feeling tired. The downside was it was highly addictive, caused users to lose a lot of weight since it took away their hunger, and made many victims look like hallowed out beings of their former selves.

I had never suspected Ronald of using shabu until one day when I arrived home from work to find that he had cleaned our apartment from top to bottom, washed all our clothes and ironed them, and cooked dinner!

"Ronald, did you really do all of this by yourself?" I asked incredulously.

"Yes, I had so much energy, and I don't even feel that tired now," he replied. My suspicions nagged me and grew even more when I began finding random pieces of aluminum foil in different parts of our apartment. Some of them bore burn marks, meaning they were used to heat up the meth before ingestion. The problem with this drug is that it apparently left no smell on users, so I never smelt it on Ronald. But this was enough for me to ask him point blank if he was using shabu.

He denied he was, and I wanted to believe him, so his denial appeased me for a while.

In November 2000, I went to Manila on vacation for a few weeks and stayed with my friend Aris. A few days before my return flight, I received a text message on my mobile from Ronald saying that some of his friends would drop off some food items for me to bring back to him. I said okay and didn't think much more about it. Two days before my flight home, I returned to Aris's house to find three large, dark glass bottles filled with coconut sweets in a syrup, that had been dropped off for me. "Gosh, these are heavy!" I said to Aris, lifting up one of the jars that must have been 30 centimeters high and weighed at least a kilo. "I can't pack these in my check-in suitcase as they could break in transit."

"Why are they sending these sweets to Ronald?" I asked Aris. "They have all of these sweets in Filipino stores in Jeddah."

On my day of departure, I suddenly decided to leave the jars with Aris.

"You and your nephews can eat the sweets," I said, not wanting to carry these huge and hefty jars with me onto the plane.

As soon as I landed in Jeddah, my phone rang while I was waiting for my suitcase to appear on the carousel.

"Do you have the sweets with you?!" asked Ronald in a strangely apprehensive voice.

"No, I left them in Manila with Aris. They were too heavy to hand carry."

When I got home, Ronald seemed very nervous but didn't tell me why.

A few days later, I got an urgent call from Aris.

"Rasheed, did you know there were drugs hidden in the jars?" said a distressed Aris.

"No, of course not!" I retorted.

"We started eating some of the sweets, and then we found some small plastic packages with white powder in them. I flushed them down the toilet," he explained. And to make matters worse, Ronald's so-called "friends" returned to Aris's house, demanding that he hand over the jars. Aris explained to them that they had eaten most of the sweets. They threatened him with violence and then left.

Aris was furious with Ronald and I. "How could Ronald do such a thing to me?!," he screamed down the phone line.

"Never come stay with me again!" he barked.

At that stage, I had known Aris for ten years and knew all of his family. I was shocked by what Ronald had done to me and Aris. But I couldn't say anything to assuage my friend's anger. Only time will heal our wounds, I thought.

I immediately broke up with Ronald. "You're such a shit,

Ronald!" I bellowed. "You could have gotten me killed! How could you have used me as a drug mule?!" It was just too much to process and comprehend. Ronald knew full well that I could have had my head chopped off if they had caught me with those drugs at the airport in Jeddah. All so that Ronald could make some side money for himself.

I immediately plunged into a deep depression. My world fell apart, and I just felt like shit. Like shit because of Ronald's callous betrayal of me, and for causing a potentially permanent rift between me and Aris.

"I don't want to see your face anymore!" I told Ronald. "Go sleep somewhere else and leave me alone."

I was so upset and distressed that I wanted to get away from Jeddah as fast as possible. At work, I took the big step of resigning. Perhaps ironically, I also began looking for a condo to rent in Makati. I was going to move to the Philippines and leave Ronald behind and all of my disgust, shame, and anger, or so I thought.

I got my end-of-service benefits payment from *Arab News*, which was the equivalent of half a month's salary for each of the first five years I worked at the paper and a whole month's pay for every year worked beyond that. I didn't have any savings, so this ESB nest egg was going to finance my move to and life in Manila.

I found a studio condo unit in Makati, the business district of Manila, and arguably the wealthiest area in the Philippines. The rent was around 13,000 pesos monthly, or U.S. $260 at 2001 exchange rates. Jazmine was the owner, and I had to give her several predated checks to cover my first six months of rent.

My friend Lito Esteban, whom I met through Amin in Saudi Arabia, was back in the Philippines and between Saudi jobs, so he moved in with me to help me settle in and keep me company. We soon joined a small gym near our apartment and became fast friends with a woman trainer there.

I arrived in Manila in December, a few weeks before Christmas. Lito was kind enough to spend Christmas with me, as none of my other friends had invited me to their celebrations. On New Year's Eve we went up to the roof of our tall building to watch the fireworks that everyone was setting off. The air was soon smoky from all the firecrackers, that Filipinos love to set off.

We ate out a lot, and I was paying for both of us, so I quickly began to worry about how long my ESB nest egg was going to last. By Saudi standards, the Philippines was a cheap country to live in, but I was no longer making my Saudi salary, so I began to look for work.

I had met Conrado de Quiros, an excellent writer and political columnist of the *Philippine Daily Inquirer*, through my fellow journalist friend Sammy Santos, who had worked for *Saudi Gazette* in Jeddah. He had introduced me to Conrad a few years earlier, and we had all gone out drinking together.

Conrad had been a speechwriter and ghostwriter for President Ferdinand Marcos, even though he was highly critical of the excesses and corruption of the Marcos regime. He was also 13 years older than me.

Conrad said I should try to get an editing job at Inq7.net, the website of the *Philippine Daily Inquirer*. I promptly wrote an email to Rigoberto Tiglao, the site's editor-in-chief, introducing myself and asking if I could work there.

Born in 1952, Tiglao had been a leftist activist during the Marcos dictatorship. He was the head of the Manila-Rizal chapter of the Communist Party of the Philippines. He and his first wife Raquel Edralin were arrested in 1973 during Martial Law and kept in prison for two years.

He later co-founded the Philippine Center for Investigative Journalism in 1989, and was the Manila bureau chief and correspondent for the *Far Eastern Economic Review* from 1989 to 2000. After his stint at Inq7.net, he moved to government, becoming the press secretary of President Gloria Macapagal-Arroyo and then was appointed Philippine ambassador to Greece. Nowadays, he's a columnist for the *Manila Times*.

But back to 2001. Tiglao promptly replied to my message, and I went in to meet him later that week in January 2001. We had a very agreeable meeting, Tiglao's curiosity perhaps piqued by meeting an Arab-American who wrote regularly about Philippine politics and culture.

I was offered a job as an online editor, with a monthly pay of 24,000 pesos, around US$480, which was considered a good salary at the time. I promptly accepted, and began going in to the office five days a week to edit stories and write my *Manila Moods* column, which Inq7.net began carrying.

Our managing editor was Gethsemane Selirio, who went by the nickname Getsy. She was nice enough, even though there was some tension between us, and I soon found out that she was secretly dating Tiglao. He was still married to Raquel, who had been battling cancer, at the time. When Raquel passed away in 2001, Tiglao and Selirio tied the knot the following year.

25
DANGERS OF WRITING FOR FOREIGN PUBLICATIONS

Both Faiza and I faced the danger of writing freely for American publications, where criticisms of Saudi Arabia were published without any censorship.

Faiza was once stopped by passport officials at Jeddah's King Abdulaziz airport when she was returning from abroad. They said that they had orders to keep her passport, which effectively meant she couldn't leave the Kingdom. She soon found out that the authorities had not liked the headline of an article she had written for *Newsweek* about the 1996 Al-Khobar bombings of US military personnel. She argued that it was her editors in New York that had put the headline on her story. She eventually got her passport back, but only after calling in favors from people who had connections with the government.

Nothing so drastic ever happened to me, thank goodness. But I did write some articles that caught the attention of the authorities. One day while having coffee with Faiza and a Saudi man who worked closely as an advisor to the government, I was startled when he casually asked me if someone in the government had gotten into contact with me about a recent story I had written that they did not like. I said "no," and left it at that.

He was clearly trying to intimidate Faiza and I, but we just laughed it off in shocked annoyance, as he clearly had no power to censor us.

I believe that Faiza and I were able to get away with writing critical stories about Saudi Arabia because we were writing in English and for foreign publications that were not widely circulated in the kingdom. The internet was still in its infancy, therefore very few people in the country had easy access to our stories. Nevertheless, we were acutely aware that the government was taking note of what we were writing, and we took the necessary precautions to write the stories we wanted but without pissing off the authorities so much that they would want to arrest us or stop us from leaving the country.

Having said that, I doubt that we could today write the same kind of stories. Any criticism of the government online has landed many Saudis in prison under the rule of Crown Prince Mohammad bin Salman. While the kingdom has opened up tremendously in the social arena, with women working, driving and not being forced to cover their hair in public, the arena for dissent has shrunk dramatically.

26

STRINGING FOR THE NYT AND ABU DHABI

In 2005, I met Hassan Fattah, the *New York Times* reporter based in Dubai. Faiza introduced me to him in Jeddah, and Fattah eventually asked me if I'd like to be a stringer for the *Times* in Saudi Arabia. I jumped at the opportunity and said yes. My job as a stringer involved interviewing Saudis for stories Fattah was writing. I enjoyed the work and seeing my name at the end of his stories that said: *"With additional reporting by Rasheed Abou-Alsamh in Jeddah."*

Fattah was an American with an Iraqi father and a Swedish mother who had grown up in California. He was short and chubby but always had a twinkle in his eye. He spoke fluent Arabic with a slight Levantine accent. We got along well, even though he had made a point of telling me at the beginning of our working relationship that I shouldn't think I could get a full-time job with the *Times*. "They never hire stringers!" a clearly happy Fattah said to me.

One time he admonished me, asking if I was improving the language of the Saudis that I was interviewing for him. "No!" I snapped back. "The people I'm interviewing are highly educated and speak excellent English," I explained. Fattah didn't think Saudis could be so polished and urbane in English.

After a few years of stringing, Fattah suddenly told me in 2007 that he was leaving Dubai and the *Times* to help establish a new English-language daily in Abu Dhabi, the capital of the United Arab Emirates. He invited me to join the paper, estimating that I would be paid US$80,000 a year, tax-free. I had never made that much money at *Arab News*, and when I asked Almaeena if he could match my offer, he said no.

27
MOVING TO ABU DHABI

Lured by the good pay and the chance to help build a newspaper from the ground up, I accepted the job offer and promptly resigned from *Arab News*.

I lived with my Filipino boyfriend Marvin then and told him he could join me later in Abu Dhabi. The new paper paid for my move, so I had my furniture, TV and other things shipped to Abu Dhabi.

I also prepared the paperwork required to bring my dog Nog-Nog with me. He was a cute mix between a terrier and a Lhasa Apso. In Saudi Arabia it was frowned upon to have dogs as pets, as they were ritually considered dirty. In Islam, one has to do a special washing if a dog licks us, before being able to pray again. And my father said that the angels would not enter my home because I had a dog.

At the airport on my way to Abu Dhabi I had to take Nog-Nog to the cargo terminal to get him scanned and put on my flight. I still remember when a Saudi customs agent asked me to take Nog-Nog out of his travel box. I pulled him out and held him up to the agent to prove that no contraband or bomb was strapped to my dear pooch! The agent shrieked in horror at seeing Nog-Nog and quickly motioned for me to return him to his carrier. I got many laughs when I later recounted the story to my friends.

I was a little apprehensive about moving to Abu Dhabi, not knowing what to expect at a new paper and in a new country.

The UAE was a British protectorate until 1971, when it gained its independence. In the 1980s, Dubai only had one skyscraper and a small airport. Just a few decades later, it would be transformed into the consumer monstrosity it is today, with its skyscrapers, huge luxury malls, and a huge, world-famous national airline.

Abu Dhabi has always been the more conservative emirate, with smaller buildings and a family atmosphere. The UAE comprises seven emirates, each with its own ruler and local regulations. While alcohol and racy nightclubs run free in Dubai, the neighboring emirate of Sharjah, for example, is dry and full of art museums.

The Emirates, unlike Saudi Arabia, are home to more foreigners than Emiratis. There are an estimated four expats for every Emirati, meaning that Dubai often seems like an Indian and Filipino city because so many of them work there.

The newspaper we were launching was *The National,* into which the ruler of Abu Dhabi had invested an estimated $100 million. It was dubbed the *New York Times* of the Gulf, and attracted Canadian, British and American journalists, eager to earn fat, tax-free salaries. Unfortunately, many of these new hires were under the false assumption that they would enjoy similar press freedoms to those they had enjoyed back home. Instead, our British editor-in-chief Martin Newland, who came from the *Daily Telegraph,* wanted our front page to be filled with utterly boring stories about how Abu Dhabi authorities were setting high standards to improve the quality of education.

I was hired as the Deputy Opinion editor, and worked under Robert Cowan, a retired older editor also from the *Daily Telegraph.* My first brush with the unique variety of Emirati censorship was when I suggested I could write an editorial about how the government could make it easier for foreigners who had worked for decades in the UAE to attain citizenship. A clearly distraught Fattah screamed "no!" and promptly shut my idea down. Years later, even the traditionally more conservative Saudi Arabia would announce that they were planning to allow Muslim expats who had lived in the kingdom a pathway if not to citizenship, then at least to permanent residency.

Many of the new recruits were young journalists in their twenties and thirties, most never having lived in the Middle East before, let alone speak Arabic. This led to some cultural misunderstandings, with the management having to send out memos warning female staff members to dress modestly while in public.

Some female staff complained of the stares they attracted from the Pakistani laborers who lived near the buildings our paper had rented out to us.

Despite these occasional challenges we managed to build and put out a new newspaper in record time, with quality international reporting, if not local stories. *The National* was soon being quoted by news agencies, and it became a widely respected newspaper. Most of the original staff is now long gone, with some ending up at the *Wall Street Journal*, *Washington Post*, NPR and other such quality media outlets.

28

THERAPY AND MOVING BACK TO BRAZIL

I began seeing a psychologist for therapy in Brasilia in 2010 for my depression. My first therapist was a Brazilian man, younger than me. I initially enjoyed our weekly sessions, but after a few months, I felt we weren't going anywhere, and I left him.

I interrupted my therapy for many years, until my mother died in 2019. Then, I found a new therapist, an older woman. Her demeanor reminded me of former Brazilian President Dilma Rousseff. She was 70 years old and was originally from Rio de Janeiro. For our sessions she would have me lie down on a chaise longue and would tell me to just talk. She took notes of what I was saying but kept her remarks and questions to a minimum. It eventually got so bad that I was spending whole sessions telling her how my life had been when I lived in Saudi Arabia. I quickly thought she should have been paying me for the information I was giving her, and not the other way around.

When I asked her to prescribe me anti-depression medication, as she was also a psychiatrist, she flatly refused, saying, "I don't believe in using medication for this." And that was the end of our professional relationship.

After my mother suddenly passed away in December 2019, I plunged into a deep depression. I would sleep all the time, and I didn't have the will to do much apart from what was utterly necessary. Luckily, my boyfriend Marcos helped me. He would see me lying on my sofa in my living room, hug me, and encourage me to get up and continue living.

I had already lost my dad and now felt like a complete orphan. My father, ten years older than my mom, became increasingly ill in 2008. He was born in Egypt in 1927 and was now 81. While I was working in Abu Dhabi, I found myself flying back to Brazil every few months to visit my parents, after my mom would send me yet another email saying my dad had been hospitalized again. In November 2008, she emailed me and told me that my dad was in the hospital once more, and that she didn't think he would last that long.

I resigned from *The National*, where I had been the Deputy Opinion editor, and moved back to Brazil. I had lived away from my parents since I was 18, and I longed to reconnect with my mother. My 20 years living in Saudi Arabia and the UAE were an imposed exile from my mother and Brazil. Moving back to Brazil wasn't that easy. At the time, Marvin, my Filipino boyfriend, was living with me in Abu Dhabi, along with my dog Nog-Nog, whom I had brought with me from Jeddah.

I convinced him to come with me, knowing I couldn't face my father's illness and probable death alone. Filipinos do not need a visa to visit Brazil, so there was no bureaucratic hurdle to tackle. Getting my furniture and appliances shipped to Brazil was going to be another thing altogether. I was returning to Brazil initially as a tourist, so I had to leave all my belongings in storage with a moving company in Abu Dhabi and pay monthly storage fees.

My parents lived in Brazil as permanent residents for years after my father retired from working for the Saudi government in the 1990s. I had to apply for permanent residency, claiming familial reunion with my mother. I only got my residency more than a year after I arrived back in Brasilia, in December 2009. In that time, I could not even open a local bank account, as I was still waiting for my residency to be approved. Then the decision to approve my residency was published in the *Diario Oficial*, and voila, I was a legal resident!

Marvin and I arrived in Brasilia on Nov. 28, 2008. I went to the HRAN hospital in the Asa Norte with my mother to visit my dad. He was in a coma and an intensive care ward with many other patients. My father had decided to stop paying for private health insurance years before this, and that is why he was being cared for in a public hospital. Brazil has the SUS medical treatment system that offers free medical care and hospitals to all Brazilians and residents. It's like the NHS in Britain.

The first time I saw my dad, his now white beard had grown out. On my next visit, a nurse had kindly shaved my father. I held my dad's hand and tried to speak to him, hoping he could somehow hear me even though he was still in a coma. I kissed his forehead, and we went home.

On the sunny morning of Dec. 2, 2008, the telephone rang at our house in the Park Way neighborhood of Brasilia. I answered it and a male voice told me that unfortunately my father had passed that night. I was shocked and cried. I then had to go out and tell my mother the news as she walked around our property.

Immediately I called Salah, my father's best friend. Salah was Egyptian but had lived for decades in Brazil working at the Kuwaiti Embassy in Brasilia. He was married to a jolly Brazilian woman from Santa Catarina, whom we had named Farida. The rest of the day was a blur as we went to the hospital to take my father's body from the morgue to the Islamic Center, where we then washed his body and wrapped him in plain cotton cloth, anointing him with his favorite cologne. We all prayed over my father's body inside the mosque, the imam leading the prayer.

We then rushed his body to the Islamic section at the Campo da Esperanca cemetery. It was now around 3 pm, and since it was summer and the rainy season, we had a massive downpour just as they were placing my father into his grave. Marvin and I got out of the car to watch. My mother, shocked, stayed in the car and watched from the window.

The Islamic exigency that a Muslim be buried as quickly as possible was being followed here. There was no embalming of the body or waiting to bury the person after one week, as is so common in the US and the Philippines.

29

MY STROKE

I never thought I would have a stroke. But on a Saturday night in early December 2022, alone at home in Houston, with my pets, I was watching a strange movie on TV when I suddenly began to feel light-headed, like I was going to faint.

I sat up on my sofa and breathed deeply, fighting the urge to slip into the darkness of unconsciousness. I knew that I couldn't blackout as I didn't know what was happening to me.

Then I felt nauseous and threw up what can only be described as something looking like very liquid coffee grounds, dark brown and granular. Then I threw up again. I tried to stand up, and I couldn't. I had lost all strength in my legs.

"That's not normal," I said to myself.

I called my cousin Kim and said with noticeable slurring "I just threw up and I feel like I'm going to pass out!"

I then called 911 and asked for an ambulance. "Help is on the way!", the operator said after taking down my address.

Within five minutes' firemen were knocking on my glass front door. With no strength in my legs to stand up, I had to drag myself across my living and dining room floors to open the door for them.

"Do you always sweat this much?", asked one of my rescuers after they sat me upright on one of my dining table chairs.

"No, of course not!", I snapped, irritated at his dumb question.

"Do you want to wait here to see if you feel better?", asked another fireman as they took an EKG of my heart.

"No, take me to the hospital!" I replied.

The white and red lights of the ambulance swirled around as I was rolled out to it, strapped down on a gurney, with only my underwear and socks on.

Once I was strapped into the ambulance, and the rescuers decided which hospital they could take me to, we sped off, bumpily, through the streets of Houston, sirens blaring, to St. Luke's Hospital in the Medical Center.

In the ER, a doctor asked me what had happened and performed some tests on me. "Can you touch the tip of my finger, and then the tip of your nose?", the doctor asked, holding up one of his fingers in front of my face.

I struggled to take my index finger and touch his fingertip, and my right arm swerved all over the place, and I found it very difficult to connect it to my nose.

The doctor immediately sent me to have a CT scan of my brain. Within minutes, he was showing me black and white images of my brain, one of them showing a darker area. "See, that's the stroke you just had," he said, showing me the screen of his phone, multiple images of my brain filling the screen, like some perverse Andy Warhol portrait.

"Do you agree to have an injection of a powerful clot-busting drug?", the doctor asked me, stressing that it would go to work quickly and that time was of the essence.

"Yes I do," I said.

. . .

The doctor administered the injection, and within a few hours I was already improving, my speech less slurry and my coordination better.

But I was still recovering, so they took me to the ICU where they could keep a close eye on me and start administering the blood thinner Eliquis to prevent another stroke from happening.

The nurses who took care of me were wonderful, especially the Filipino ones, who chatted with me about the Philippines and brought me graham crackers and vanilla pudding as snacks.

Houston is a cosmopolitan melting pot, attracting people from all around the world. I had a male nurse named Kennedy, originally from Nigeria, and another nurse from Tanzania.

After the initial shock of having a stroke wore off and I felt assured that I was in good hands, I began to worry about who was going to feed my two dogs and three cats. I messaged Kim and asked her to feed them and let my dogs out in my backyard. Thankfully, she agreed and took good care of my furry ones.

On my third day in the hospital, a senior doctor came around with interns and watched them as they asked me questions about how my stroke had happened.

After they had finished quizzing me, the senior doctor said, "You're on the young side of old to be having a stroke. We need to find the root cause of your stroke before you go home."

Later that day I was finally taken downstairs on a bed to have an echocardiogram done. As the technician spread gel on my chest, she began moving the wand on it, sending waves into my body, taking photos of the images it produced.

Near the end, a doctor took over, instructing the technician to push saline solution through the access in my hand. He then squeezed my upper right arm and looked at the screen to see if any bubbles were produced in my heart.

Nothing was said to me at that moment. I was taken back to my room and waited for the doctor, who said I would be discharged that night, to return and tell me the results of my test.

The dinner service came at 5:15 p.m. There was still no sign of the doctor. So I ate my meal and waited. Finally, at around 7 p.m., he came rushing in, saying that I had a patent foramen ovale (PFO) in my heart. He said it was a small flap opening between the two chambers of the heart that every baby has it while in the womb. The opening usually closes on its own before birth or shortly thereafter. But for one in four people, this opening never closes.

Most people do not realize they have the opening, and may never find out, unless they suffer a stroke like I did. The opening is where the blood clot probably formed and traveled to my brain, causing the stroke, explained the doctor, practically running out of my room without calmly discussing treatment options with me.

I was a little surprised that the doctor dropped this bombshell and then ran off! But I was relieved that at least we had a reasonable explanation of what had happened to me and why.

In January 2023 I had a small medical device implanted into my heart by Dr. Pranav Loyolka. He accessed my heart through a vein in my groin area, and pushed the device, folded up, through a tube threaded through my vein into my heart. Once inside my heart, the device was deployed, opening up, and positioned to close the hole.

Weeks later another echocardiogram showed that the device was still in place. My doctor said that my heart would grow tissue around it, further holding it in place. I was amazed at the wonders of modern medicine!

30
1983: THE YEAR EVERYTHING CHANGED

My father loved shocking Jamelah and me with lurid descriptions of sex. I guess it was his form of sex ed.

After he saw "Last Tango in Paris" in 1972, the steamy Bernardo Bertolucci film starring Marlon Brando and Maria Schneider, he said, "The movie is bad. It shows Brando screwing the woman using butter as a lubricant!"

I was only 8 years old, and my sister was 13, so we didn't have any idea what having sex was about, or at least I didn't.

Another time he said: "These homosexuals screw each other in the bottom because the penetration of the penis and rubbing of the prostate is what gives them pleasure!" I don't know why he felt compelled to describe such a gay act in so much detail. Had he sensed that I was going to be gay when I grew up? Was it because I was somewhat effeminate and always preferred to be around my mother and sister, instead of doing "manly" things?

I don't think he could blame me, as he spent our years in Geneva and Brasilia busy with work all the time. Our mother was the one who stayed home with us and took us out shopping.

"Stop daddy!" I said. "We don't want to hear this!" I would protest.

"But you have to know these things," he replied.

I think my father was at once both horrified and entranced by what he viewed to be the moral decadence of Western society. He would always tell us how Muslim women were allowed to own property, centuries before women were in the West. For him this was proof of Islam's moral superiority to Christianity and Judaism.

When I finally reached Swarthmore College in the Fall of 1983, I felt elated at all the possibilities American freedom of expression had in store.

My father took me to the campus to see me settle into my dorm room in Mertz, a rather bland dorm built in the 1970s. Unlike American students who came by car from Pennsylvania or New York, I didn't bring furniture, mini-fridges, or large pillows with me. I only had my suitcase, clothes, passport, and cash. Mertz had none of the charm of the much older main buildings on campus, which were from the late 1800s and early 1900s.

The campus was stunningly beautiful. Expansive manicured lawns stretched out, with many trees and flowers planted by the Scott Arboretum, part of the college. The main building, Parrish Hall, was set on a hill above the train station and the village of Swarthmore. Like the White House in Washington, it had burned down and been rebuilt. Swamp white oaks lined Magill Walk from Parrish to the train station. Redwoods and beech trees also populated the campus.

We were only 12 miles outside Philadelphia but seemed removed from the everyday world. At Swarthmore, we were in a bubble of exacting academics and the Quaker values of peace and always helping the oppressed. It was also one of the rare colleges in the late 1890s to have been founded as co-educational, a rarity at the time. Our nearby Quaker sister schools, Bryn Mawr and Haverford, were initially established as women's and men's colleges. They, too, would later become co-ed.

My dad decamped rather quickly and left me to meet my roommate Andrew, who was from a Quaker family but liked to smoke weed. We got along until he got a girlfriend, Sylvia, and they began having sex in his bed, with the lights out, with me in my bed. It was gross for me as a sexual neophyte. I soon applied to move to a single room, citing irreconcilable differences with Andrew. He eventually moved out, and I, much to my relief, had the room all to myself for the rest of the year.

For entertainment, my new friend Michael and I soon found out that there was a mall near our campus. Springfield Mall was a brisk 20-minute walk from Swarthmore and had all the stores and ATMs that suburban malls had at the time. We would buy clothes and music there. On Oct. 30, 1985, when we were sophomores, a mentally ill young woman named Sylvia Seegrist drove to the mall in her Datsun and took out a rifle and began shooting at people first outside, and then inside the mall. She was eventually overpowered and rendered by a graduate student, but not before killing three people and wounding seven others.

The news shocked us, and thankfully no one from Swarthmore was affected by the shootings. After a while we returned to the mall, and I remember the huge dent left in the metal casing of the ATM that a bullet shot by Seegrist hit. She had been aiming at a woman in the parking lot but thankfully missed and instead hit the ATM. Seegrist received three consecutive life terms and is still alive today in prison. When she was asked by a mall security guard why she had done the shootings, Seegrist replied: "My family makes me nervous."

At this same mall during my first semester at Swarthmore, I got my first ear piercing. I had thought about it beforehand, sure that my dad would freak out if he saw me wearing an earring. At the time, there was an urban legend circulating that said men getting their right ear pierced meant they were gay, and if you got your left ear pierced, that just meant you were hip. But to my dad that didn't matter. For him only females got pierced. It was a strict no-no for men.

I had only recently become aware of the signaling that some gay men gave each other by the color of their bandanas and on which side of their back jeans pocket they tied them to. One side meant you were passive, the other side meant you were a top. I did not use bandanas, but it certainly was an introduction to the semiotics of the gay world. "I'm scared of my dad's reaction," I told Michael. "But I want to have an earring."

It's laughable now, 41 years later, but at the time, it was a monumental decision that I had to make. I felt very nervous, knowing that my pierced ear would be a shot across the bow of my dad's homophobic fears. In Muslim countries, baby girls often got their ears pierced as a statement to the world that they are female and not male. It was a practice that had deep roots in Islamic culture.

When I finally convinced myself that I would get it done, I walked over to the mall and asked a young woman at a stall selling gold ear studs to please pierce my left ear. She quickly disinfected my ear lobe with an alcohol pad, and drew the spot with a marker where the hole would go.

"Does that look okay," she asked me, while holding up a hand mirror for me to see the spot.

"Yes, that's fine," I replied.

I closed my eyes as the woman raised the ear punching device to my earlobe. I felt a quick pinch and then I had a gold stud in my earlobe!

I felt a rush of euphoria. "Finally! My earlobe is pierced!" I thought to myself. This simple act of rebellion elated and scared me at the same time.

The woman sent me back to campus with strict instructions

not to remove the stud for several weeks, or else my hole would close. She also said I had to disinfect my earlobe with a cotton ball soaked in rubbing alcohol several times a day to avoid infection. Back on campus, most students didn't notice that I had pierced my ear. "That's exactly the reaction I wish my family and relatives would have," I said. But just like Seegrist, my family made me nervous.

I got increasingly anxious as my Christmas break drew closer. I was flying home to Brasilia and would have to face my parents' reaction to my pierced ear.

"Do you think I should just take it out for the holiday, and put back in when I return to Swarthmore?" I asked Michael.

"Maybe. But just do what you want," was his reply.

My stomach was in knots as I took the train to New York where I would catch my flight back to Brazil from John F. Kennedy airport. My nerves gave me diarrhea; my fears were so big.

I barely slept on the flight down, and upon arriving in Brasilia, I found both my father and mother waiting to pick me up at the airport.

"What's that on your ear!" my mother hissed into my ear as we hugged.

"It's just an earring," I said.

My father didn't say anything, and we were enveloped in icy silence as we drove home.

"Perhaps dad doesn't mind?" I asked myself rather disingenuously.

As soon as we got home, all hell broke loose! My dad and mom both started to shout at me, asking why I had pierced my ear.

"Are you a homosexual?!" my dad raged, his eyes looking as if they might pop out of his head. "Was it that English teacher of yours at EAB? Did he make you gay?"

He was referring to Dr. C, a camp teacher of mine who EAB had hired after fleeing Iran in 1979 with his wife, where they had been teaching at the Tehran American School.

"The school board received complaints about him from parents, saying he was gay," my dad explained to me.

"No, of course not," I replied, appalled that he could think a single teacher could brainwash me and make me gay.

"Many men are wearing earrings nowadays," I tried to meekly explain to both of them.

"It no longer means you're gay if you have one."

My parents were not buying anything I was saying.

"It's a disease!" exclaimed my mother. "You need to see a psychiatrist to cure you of this," she added.

Both had burst into tears. I had never seen my father cry before and was rather shocked at the sight.

"If you continue to be gay, you cannot go back to the US," my dad threatened. "I'm so upset that I want to kill myself, but I can't as suicide is sinful in Islam," he explained. "I think I should kill you!" he exclaimed, looking at me.

They eventually banished me to my room, saying I could only come out if I took my earring out.

It was 1983, I was 19 years old, and there were no cellphones back then, and I didn't have any gay friends in Brasilia, apart from Alisson, whom I could talk to. So, I stayed in my room with a small bathroom attached to it. My mother would bring me food on a tray. I was a hostage in my childhood home, with my parents as my captors.

I felt emotionally drained. While essential, fighting for your essence and existence was tiring and depressing. I just slept night and day, cocooned in my bedroom, with the only light coming from my desk lamp beside my bed.

One day, I awoke abruptly to see my dad removing a handgun from the drawer of my desk, right next to my head. I recoiled in fear. "Is he going to kill me right here? Shoot me in my bed?!" I thought.

Much later, he told me that he had been occasionally sleeping in my bed while I was away, and that the gun was there as protection from potential intruders.

After four days of being held captive, I gave in and took my stud out. I couldn't stand being held prisoner in my room any longer.

"I'm not gay any longer," I announced to my parents in the living room, showing them my now empty earlobe.

It was the only way I knew how to break the impasse. I knew then that I could never convince my parents that it was okay for me to be gay. And I needed to go back to Swarthmore and complete my degree. I knew I was lying to my parents, and they were so desperate to believe me that they did.

It would be another 13 years before my dad asked me again about my being gay.

31
FALLOUT FROM LOVING A NARCISSIST

I had always thought that battered women who kept going back to their male abusers were weak in a fundamental way. How could a sane person willingly submit themselves to more abuse? Abuse that often ended in death when their abuser killed them.

What I didn't realize was that many people return to their abusers because they lack outside support to be able to leave them, and because of financial and emotional reasons. Being literally addicted to the person that caused them so much mental anguish, shame and sometimes physical pain, meant that they crumbled and were lured right back in when their abusers lavished them with love words and appeals for forgiveness.

My relationship with Lorenzo was like that. He abused me and instead of leaving him I would always return to him. I rationalized away his bad behavior, which he happily helped me do by blaming others. He was a master manipulator, so much so that I only left him after he robbed my mother's jewelry and left my house turned upside down.

It took 11 years of continued mental, financial, and emotional abuse, and five years of therapy after the end of our relationship, to finally wake up and admit to myself that Lorenzo did NOT love me or want the best for me.

This was a hard realization for me to come to, as I was always thrilled when Lorenzo would message or call me on WhatsApp after he had committed another crime against me or my mother.

The first crime he committed against me was in 2012, when, unbeknownst to me, he listed me as a financial guarantor on his application to rent an apartment in Guara, a suburb of Brasilia. The flat's owner called me in 2013, telling me that Lorenzo was several months behind on his rent.

"What does that have to do with me?" I asked.

"You signed as his guarantor on the rental agreement," the man said.

"No! I never signed such a paper, and Lorenzo never asked me to do this for him," I practically yelled down the line, livid at such a betrayal.

"Your signature was verified at the *cartorio*," he added.

"Why didn't you bother calling me to confirm if I was indeed his guarantor before renting the apartment to Lorenzo?" I asked, indignant at such a lapse.

Lorenzo later sheepishly admitted to me that he had desperately put me down as his guarantor. When renting an apartment in Brasilia, the lessor usually asks for at least two financial guarantors to cover possible unpaid rent. And also so that they can sue them later in court if things go south.

And that is precisely what happened. The apartment owner sued both Lorenzo and I for the unpaid rent, of course adjusted with late fees and interest. I hired two lawyers to defend me in court and prove I had never signed the blasted rental agreement.

On the day of the court hearing in front of the female judge, I sat on one side of the table with my lawyers, and Lorenzo sat on the other side with his lawyer. I stated that I had never signed the document, and my lawyers asked that my signature be proved false. The judge agreed and ordered me to go to a court-appointed handwriting expert to verify my claim.

I had to pay the equivalent of US $1,000 to the expert out of my pocket. On the designated day, I went to the expert's office. He was a large, jolly fellow who asked me to copy some text down in my handwriting. Then, he asked me to sign my full name so many times that my right hand was left aching at the end.

After a few weeks past, the expert's report came out saying that he didn't think I had signed the lease. I was elated with the result, and the judge struck me from the lawsuit against Lorenzo. I felt relieved and vindicated.

Much worse news was to come in February 2013 when Lorenzo told me with great difficulty that he had something important to tell me.

"What is it?" I asked.

We were at our favorite café where we would meet several times a week to drink *cafezinhos* (espressos), *agua com gas* (bubbly mineral water) and eat pastries, all while talking about politics and the economy.

"I'm sorry I'm only telling you this now, but my first son was born yesterday," he said, looking at me sheepishly.

"What?! You have a son?! With whom?" I asked.

"With Tatiana. I've been living with her since last year," he replied.

I was so shocked I couldn't say anything for a minute. I had known that Lorenzo was bisexual and that Tatiana was a girlfriend from before he met me. But to get married to her and not tell me anything? I couldn't muster the words; I was gob smacked.

When I finally regained the ability to speak, I said: "And where does that leave us? Does she know about us?"

"You have the choice of leaving me now, or we can continue on as things are," he explained, sounding as if it would be the easiest decision in the world for me to make.

And why did I have to decide? Why didn't he have the decency to tell me that he was moving in with Tatiana and was going to have a family with her, I thought, my mind racing.

"I need some time to think about this," I said, getting up and going home.

Unfortunately for me, a few days later I said I wanted to continue with him, too weak to break up with him. Perhaps the sex with him was so wonderful that I was willing to be the "second wife", his lover, while his wife and kid waited for him to come home every night.

I clung to Lorenzo because of his muscled arms, his height of six feet, his very large cock, smooth skin, and slight native Indian features that so-called *caboclos* have in Brazil, and his ability to seduce me with just a few words. I loved the sound of his voice, the way he laughed when we would joke around. I also liked the way he shouted at people in public when he got angry at them, and all the swear words that he peppered his Portuguese with. It was thrilling for me, so much so that I too started using these same swear words while speaking to other Brazilians. He would regularly exclaim "*porra!*" and "*caralho!*", which when translated literally mean "cum" and "cock" in English.

These were not words used in polite society.

I think I adored him so much because he reminded me of my dad. Lorenzo was masculine in all the ways I wasn't. That was a definite turn-on, and something I longed for in the men I had relationships with. I was tired of the rather effeminate Filipino boyfriends I had had so far.

And the sex was like being in a gay porn movie. I must say that Brazilian men are the best lovers I have ever encountered.

"What is this? 'Amor de *piroca*'?! exclaimed Ricky to me one day when I brought Lorenzo up.

That meant "love of cock" in Portuguese. And yes, it did seem that Lorenzo had thoroughly seduced me with his physical attributes and personality.

But Lorenzo wasn't done disappointing me. In 2014, I was planning to register a small LLC company in my name, with Lorenzo as my partner in the business. It would deal with journalistic projects and the like. On the day that I was going to my accountant to sign the papers, a woman appeared at our front gate. When I went to see who it was, I saw a white, upper middle-class woman with a darker woman who looked like a maid.

"How can I help you?" I asked, my antennae already alarmed that this had something to do with Lorenzo.

"Do you know a Lorenzo?" asked the white woman.

"Yes, I do. Why do you ask?" I replied.

"He befriended this woman here who is my cleaner and promised her he would marry her and live with her. He took all her life savings and disappeared with her money! Now we are trying to track him down," she said.

I gasped.

"I'm sure you know him. He's tall, handsome and has those beefy arms," the cleaning lady said.

"We met at the bus stop down there one day and we dated. I gave him R$50,000 (the equivalent of around US$10,000), all the money I had saved my entire life, to buy a house for us to live in together. Then he disappeared with my money and is hiding from me," she told me.

I was aghast at hearing this news. The woman was not attractive, well over 50, and couldn't be the type of woman that Lorenzo would fall for.

"I haven't seen Lorenzo for a few days," I told them before they left.

I was shocked and felt completely humiliated hearing how Lorenzo had ripped off a poor woman. I immediately called Lorenzo for an explanation. He claimed he had returned the money to the woman after the real estate deal had collapsed. That didn't make me feel better, but his seemingly rational explanation for his misdeed allowed me to once again push this one to the back of my brain.

I then called my accountant and told him to strike Lorenzo as my partner in the company. Lorenzo was outraged when he found out later, but I told him I couldn't fully trust him after that incident.

And Lorenzo, once again, wasn't done with his misdeeds and shenanigans. Around two years later, my mother received a phone call from the owner of a small real estate office, saying that the rent was overdue for a property in which she was listed as a guarantor. He had struck again!

I went to the office the next day to meet the owner and find out what was going on.

"Look at this contract. Your mother is listed and here is her signature on the document," said the elderly owner showing me the contract.

Indeed, her name and Brazilian ID number were there. But the signature was a total mess. It didn't look anything close to my mom's real signature. It looked like a 9-year-old had tried to copy my mom's handwriting.

"This signature is fake!" I said.

"And who is this woman who rented the apartment? We have never heard of her before," I added, pointing to the contract.

I would later find out that the woman was a girlfriend of Lorenzo, whom he claimed was his cousin.

Luckily, the owner believed me and said that they would investigate. A few days later I took my mother to the police station next to the Mane Garincha soccer stadium, to file a police report against Lorenzo.

That was stressful for me and embarrassing. "How could I have such bad taste in men that I had exposed my mother and her name to fraud?!" I thought. But my mother was strangely silent and did not berate me for dating Lorenzo. That was a relief, but perhaps a mistake on my mother's part. Maybe if she had raised a stink, I would have snapped out of my brainwashed veneration of Lorenzo, that caused me to make up excuses for him each time he screwed up.

He had not yet stolen money from me or my mother, but little did I know that he had bigger things planned for us.

After my mother passed away in December 2019, following a botched heart procedure, I was plunged into a deep depression. I couldn't get up off of my couch in my living room and wanted to constantly take naps. The woman with whom I had lived with for the past 11 years, was suddenly gone. Who would I have breakfast and lunch with every day? Who would I watch CNN and BBC News on TV in the evenings? Life had lost most of its meaning for me.

I was in the hospital when my mom passed. She had been placed in an intensive care unit, induced into a coma, and intubated. She lasted for around four days. On her second day in the ICU, I was woken up at 2:30 am by a call from the doctor on duty at the hospital.

"Why aren't you here by your mother's side?" she asked me in an accusatory tone. There was no bed in her room for me to sleep on, and I was going to see her every day during the daytime.

"Please come in right away so I can talk with you about her condition," snapped the doctor.

I immediately got dressed and drove to the hospital, mad at the doctor for calling me at such an ungodly hour and scaring me! I thought my mom had passed away and that she was calling me to tell me.

When I got to the hospital the doctor said my mother was stable and did not have much news to tell me.

On the fourth day, I drove to the hospital and arrived at around 9:15 am. I checked on my mother and held her hand. I then went to a waiting area at the entrance to the ICU unit to call friends. I asked them to come and keep me company. Several were already there, and more were coming.

I was talking with my dear childhood friend Gitty, when a nurse quickly came over to us.

"I'm so sorry. Your mother didn't resist and has just passed away," she told us.

I immediately shot up and started walking to her room. The nurse ran after me, saying, "Please wait. They are taking the tube out of her mouth and cleaning up a bit before you can see her."

I waited around ten minutes and went in to see my mom laying in her hospital bed. Her eyes closed; the color drained from her face. I immediately began crying and I clutched Gitty.

"I don't want to continue living!" I wailed through tears. "I want to go with her!"

The rest of the morning was rather a blur. More friends soon showed up. Ricky offered to put my mother's dentures back into her mouth. Our old maid Nilda cried at my mom's bedside holding her hand, saying "How terrible that you are gone! I will never forget you! I love you!"

Abduallah, a Brazilian friend of mine, and a convert to Islam, quickly shot into action, phoning the imam at the Islamic Center to tell him of the death and arrange for a funeral prayer that afternoon. He also called a Brazilian Muslim woman to come and do the ritual washing of my mom's body before wrapping her in a plain white cloth, as is done for all Muslims.

In Islam, it is customary to bury the deceased as fast as possible. No more than 24-hours should pass between a person's death and their burial. Thus, there is no embalming industry in Islam like there is in America, where deceased relatives can be kept from decaying for weeks sometimes as relatives come from far-flung places for their funeral. I was relieved that my mother was not going to be embalmed, as I had seen too many episodes of "Six Feet Under," and found the practice of draining bodies of blood and then pumping them with formaldehyde rather gruesome.

All the preparations had to be made right away. I think I was running on pure adrenaline that day to get everything done in time. My mother died on a Saturday morning, and the cemetery workers would be there only until 6pm. On Sundays no one was buried in Brasilia.

First, I had to get a death certificate, then go to the cemetery and pay for the plot that my mother would be buried in. My friend Ana Claudia accompanied me to get these tasks done. We quickly ate lunch at a nearby restaurant and then had to rush across town back to hospital to accompany my mother's body to the mosque for her funeral prayer, and then to the cemetery for burial.

When we got back to the hospital my mom was washed, perfumed, and wrapped, ready to be taken to the mosque. Workers from the cemetery showed up with a plain, white coffin in which to carry my mother downstairs to their vehicle.

We took a special elevator that went directly to the underground parking lot. As we were wheeling her coffin on a gurney to the small truck that would carry her to the mosque, my phone rang. It was my nephew Alex, the son of Jamelah, calling from Michigan.

"I'm sorry that your mom passed away," Alex told me. "I was just calling to see how you're doing," he added.

I was in too much of a daze to deal with him and told him I couldn't talk right now.

Arriving at the mosque, my mother's temporary coffin was placed in front of where the imam usually stands. I looked around and saw the Egyptian imam, who came over and gave me his condolences.

I also saw that many Brazilian women friends of my mother had showed up to honor her. These were women that my mother had known at the International Women's Club and the ones who came to our house every Monday afternoon for English conversation with my mother. They all had covered their hair and were teary eyed. It pleased me to see that my mother had been so loved by these ladies.

The funeral prayer only took around ten minutes. My eyes swelled with tears, recognizing the Arabic words that had also been said at my father's and my grandmother's funerals. Despite my sadness, there was some comfort going through these motions. These traditions brought some semblance of order to an otherwise bewildering and chaotic event.

And then we were off to the cemetery. There a large hole had been dug in the Muslim section where my father had been buried years earlier. It had been a sunny day, and the sun was beginning to set.

Abdullah asked me if I could jump into the burial hole to help position my mother's body correctly, but I declined, saying I wasn't physically able. He jumped in and positioned my mother's body, while pulling apart her shroud at her face, telling me that Muslims had to be buried in such a fashion. He was a practicing and religious Muslim, so I accepted what he said.

He climbed out of the hole and recited a burial prayer in Arabic, and I threw some handfuls of dirt on her body. My eyes were filled with tears, and the world became a blur in front of me. We then watched the grave diggers fill in the hole with the earth that they had only been recently shoveled out.

I walked out of the cemetery arm-in-arm with my friend Camille

Lenox. She tried to console with me soothing words, but I can't remember what she said to me. I was in a daze of grief and drove myself home.

All I wanted to do now was lie down in my living room and try to distract myself with some television. My brain couldn't take remembering all that had happened that day. I wanted to forget everything and pretend that I would eat breakfast the next morning with my mother as we had always done.

32
PROUDLY BETWEEN TWO WORLDS

Nearly six years after my mother's sudden death I have been able to rebuild my life, leaving behind the immense grief that haunted me through the pandemic. It wasn't easy. Most days I did just the necessary to pay the bills, keep my house clean and take care of my dogs and cats.

With my depression I just wanted to lie down on my sofa and take long naps. It was my way of dealing with the grief of loss. One day my mom was there, the next she wasn't. She had predicted that I would sell her *chacara* soon after her death, and I did. The place reminded me of her and of her absence everywhere I looked.

Moving to Houston was not easy. I had to go through all of my parents' things, burning old bills and documents that they had saved for decades. My therapist Regina came over and helped me go through my mother's clothes. She took large bags of them to a church charity that would pass them on to people in need. But even then, I held on to a whole closet full of my mom's clothes that I brought with me to Texas. Only now, four years after my move, have I decided to take her remaining clothes to Goodwill.

Holding on to her clothes was my way of remaining close to her memory. But as Regina told me more than once, my mother would live on forever in my heart and memory. I didn't need her clothes for that.

My most fond memories of my mother, father and sister are when we lived in Geneva, Switzerland. It was the 1970s and we were living in freedom and happiness. My mom positively glowed in her beauty and grace, my dad was dashingly handsome, and my sister and I were happy with our friends, family life and days at school.

Being Third Culture kids, we were citizens of the world. We spoke English at home, French on the streets and overheard Arabic every day when my dad spoke on the phone with friends and colleagues. We had my mother's Christian traditions of celebrating Christmas, which she was quite fond of, and learned about Islamic history and traditions from our dad.

My parents sent me to the Swiss public school up the hill from our apartment for first grade so that I could learn to speak and write in French. After that I studied at various international schools in English, going back to that same Swiss public school for the fifth grade, the year before we moved to Brazil.

Living and working in Saudi Arabia introduced me to the Philippines and its people and culture. If I had never lived in the kingdom, I doubt I would have fallen in love with Philippine history and its people the way I did.

Moving back to Brazil in 2008 and living there with my mother until 2019, reunited me with the country, its people, its language, and most of all to her.

I say reunited with my mother because I had never returned to live with my parents since the age of 18 when I left to study Arabic in Saudi Arabia and then study at Swarthmore College for four years. Sure, I would occasionally go home to visit them, but I'd only stay for a few weeks at time, at most a month. And when I was working in Saudi, I saw my parents even less. In fact, I would see my dad more than my mom, as he would regularly come to Jeddah to visit his siblings, leaving my mom alone in Brasilia.

And I, instead of going to Brazil for my annual vacation, would opt to go to Manila to visit my Filipino friends. There I could be myself, and I was accepted. Back in Brasilia, my parents never fully embraced me for who I was.

But I try not to hold grudges against them. They gave me and my sister wonderful lives, full of everything we needed and excellent educations. They were from a different era, and the clash of different cultures produced situations that, especially my father, could not cope with.

My being gay and my sister running away for her freedom were shocks to my parents. I still believe that Jamelah could have gotten what she wanted from life if she had stayed with us and fought for her beliefs. Today she might still be alive, married to a Brazilian man, who could have converted to Islam to please my father, and had Brazilian children. But that's just my wishful thinking.

I have strived for decades to write conscientiously as a journalist and as a citizen of this world, trying to bridge the gaps between cultures by explaining each side to the other. This reached its apex with my *O Globo* column about Saudi Arabia and the Arab world. I explained to a lay Brazilian audience what was happening in the Middle East and why. And I didn't sugarcoat things. I criticized the unacceptable and praised the achievements.

In the end, my sister and I were products of the 1960s and 1970s. We were liberal progressives, who grew up listening to Martin Luther King's "I Have a Dream" speech at school, and rubbing shoulders with people of all nationalities and religions. We were the original globalists, that Republicans love to bash today.

I don't care what they say. The world needs more globalists and less narrow-minded partisans who think they are the greatest. I'm proud to be a globalist who has succeeded in improving the cross-border sharing of knowledge and culture. And I hope that through my writing and friendships I have been able to do just that.

THANK YOU FOR READING

I hope you have enjoyed reading my memoir. Please leave a review on Amazon, or wherever you bought my book. It will help other readers find out about my book. Thank you!
—**Rasheed Abou-Elsamh**
www.rasheedsworld.com

Acknowledgments

Thanks to my writing workshop at **Grackle & Grackle** in Houston, and in particular to **Georgina Key**, for encouraging me to finish the manuscript and for your constructive feedback.

Thanks to **Ricky Seabra** for our daily WhatsApp video calls. You kept me going when I was blue.

Thanks to **Aris Anonas** for always being such a good friend.

Thanks to **Julie Javellana** and **Narciso Chan** for their support and encouragement of my coverage of the Philippines.

Thanks to my therapist **Regina**, who helped me put the pieces back together after my mother's death in 2019.

Thanks to all of my Brazilian and Filipino friends who have always been able to make me laugh and feel at home.

Finally, thanks to my mom, **Joyce Storkson**, who helped me with my writing since I was a child. Without you this would not have been possible.

www.ingramcontent.com/pod-product-compliance
Lightning Source LLC
Chambersburg PA
CBHW040235110526
44582CB00018B/199